Tanganyika

3

‡‡‡‡‡‡‡‡‡‡‡‡‡ *National Planning Series* ‡‡‡‡‡‡‡‡‡‡‡‡‡
BERTRAM M. GROSS, GENERAL EDITOR
‡‡‡

Tanganyika
Preplanning

FRED G. BURKE

Preface by
BERTRAM M. GROSS

SYRACUSE UNIVERSITY PRESS

First Edition 1965

Acknowledgment

This and other volumes in the National Planning
Series were initiated with the encouragement and
support of Stephen K. Bailey, Dean of the Maxwell
Graduate School of Citizenship and Public Affairs,
Syracuse University, and of his predecessor, Harlan
Cleveland. They have been made possible through
a grant from the Ford Foundation for cross-cultural
research by the Maxwell School. In the final editing
of the manuscript valuable assistance was provided
by Sherry Siracuse and James Gies.

BERTRAM M. GROSS

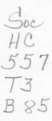

Manufactured in the United States of America

For Becky

‡‡

Acknowledgments

The material for this study was gathered over a four-year period. A number of graduate students in Syracuse University's Program of Eastern African Studies have contributed at various stages to the gathering and analysis of data. I am particularly indebted to Anthony Rweyemamu, now lecturing in political science at the University College, Dar es Salaam, and to Thomas Rasmussen. Edward Cunningham long-time friend, former district officer in the Uganda Civil Service, and subsequently a graduate of the Harvard School of Business Administration, made a major contribution to this study, here and in the United Kingdom. The Cross Cultural Study Project of Syracuse University's Maxwell Graduate School of Citizenship and Public Affairs provided financial assistance. I am particularly indebted to Mr. Bertram Gross who not only is responsible for the project of which this study is a part, but who also talked through with me many of the ideas herein contained.

F. G. B.

Contents

The Gamesmanship of National Planning

Geographers in Afric maps
With savage pictures fill their gaps
And o'er unhabitable downs
Place elephants for want of towns . . .
JONATHAN SWIFT, "On Poetry, a Rhapsody"

Although geographers have done better since Swift wrote these lines in the eighteenth century, American ignorance of Africa has long been widespread and deep. Most people have only had such vaguely romantic pictures of the Dark Continent as Mt. Kilimanjaro capped with snow.

However, Fred Burke is one of the small group of American scholars who concerned themselves with Africa before the 1960 big-power conflict in the Congo suddenly awakened American policymakers to the importance of Africa. Since then, he has been developing an approach to African studies based on the following guidelines: (1) *live in Africa;* (2) *develop an interdisciplinary team* (which Burke has done both in the faculty of his East African studies program and in the composition of the eight-man group of students preparing doctoral dissertations in Tanganyika); (3) *work intimately with Africans* (as illustrated by the fact that a Tanzanian was the first to complete his dissertation [1] under this

---

[1] Anthony Hubert Rweyemamu, "Nation-Building and the Planning Processes in Tanzania" (unpublished doctoral dissertation, Graduate School of Syracuse University, September 1965).

program, and (4) *gain perspective by looking at the rest of the world also* (which Burke accomplishes by playing an active role in international studies of national planning and local government).

If this historical study deals with *pre*planning, it may also be regarded as essential *pre*research. It raises many important questions for those now conducting or planning research in Tanzania, East Africa, and Africa as a whole. Indeed, it illustrates the need for historical research as a rich background to the study of current national planning in any country—whether pre-industrial or industrial, communist or noncommunist.

Nevertheless, Burke touches a number of vital themes of *immediate* interest to national leaders involved in what he calls "the international gamesmanship of national planning" (p. 58). Among these are the role of pre-industrial countries in big-power conflict, the conflict between nation-building and transnational system-building, the local-national network of political power, and the wreckage and by-products of grandiose plans such as Britain's "groundnut scheme." These are themes that must be handled in subsequent studies of present-day Tanzanian planning. They are relevant to national planning in all Africa—and, indeed, to Asia, the Middle East, and Latin America, as well. They have a major bearing on the critical problems of North America and Europe in adjusting to their minority status in a world population becoming increasingly "non-white." Accordingly, I shall comment briefly on these themes in the broader context of national planning processes throughout the world.

FROM DIVIDE-AND-RULE TO DIVIDE-AND-DEVELOP

Long before Columbus set sail for America, the Arabs and the Portuguese probed into Africa below the Saharan desert, the Africa of the Negroes. Over the course of the centuries "civilization" was brought to black Africa by the Spanish, Dutch, Belgian, French, Italian, German, and British colonists. "Civilization" was a strange compound of (1) a little modern medicine, education, public works, and consumer goods, (2) missionaries and Christianity on a somewhat larger scale, (3) still larger-scale plundering of African resources, (4) recurring bloodshed, and (5) three or four centuries during which the decline of European serfdom was followed by the rise of African slavery.[2] In looking back upon this turbulent period of African colonialism, one finds a confusing balance sheet of gains and losses for both sides. These will be debated for centuries. Yet one fact is unmistakable: during the period of colonialism Africa was helplessly fought over by external rulers. By the end of the nineteenth-century, divide-and-rule became the jungle code of the imperial powers. "Divide" had two aspects. In order to rule without too many wars among themselves, the imperialists partitioned the vast African territories into possessions, protectorates, and spheres of influence. In order to prevent rebellion by the ruled, they fostered internal divisions among the Africans. As Burke points out, "the creation, or perpetuation, of tribal, regional, or other spatial or ethnic differences, provided a form of internal tension that could be manipulated to insure continued control and contribute to a capacity to cope with isolated incidents of rebellion" (p. 24). These policies were so successful that "had anyone suggested in 1946 that Tanganyika would be self-governing in 1961, he would have been thought mad" (p. 41).

Divide-and-become free, in contrast, has long been the operational code of oppressed people seeking freedom from tyranny. The American revolutionaries in 1776 could hardly have thrown off the British yoke unless they succeeded in playing the French against the British. Similarly, the spectacular—and relatively bloodless—victories of the African independence leaders stemmed not only from "the black man's long-standing irritation with his subordinate status" but from "the postwar emergence of a world situation conducive to changing it. . . . The *élan* of African 'nationalism' is in part a whirlwind set in motion by a bipolar world balance of power" (p. 43). Burke refers, of course, to the bipolarization between the communist nations led by the Soviet Union and

[2] The large-scale American import of African slaves during the eighteenth and early nineteenth centuries led to a central issue in the American Civil War of 1860–65. A hundred years later, the descendants of the slaves had still not won the full constitutional rights or economic and social opportunities that had been promised them. Yet the rapid progress made as a result of the "Negro revolt" of the last few years has been unquestionably due, at least in part, to the example set by the progressive elimination of colonial rule in Africa and the emergence of African leaders on the world stage.

the noncommunist nations led by the United States. The African leaders did not create the cold war nor do very much to bring it to Africa. What they did was capitalize upon this sharp division among the external powers in order to win their political freedom. By a great historic role reversal they took over divide-and-rule for their own purposes—not to rule others but to win freedom for ruling themselves.

But once freedom from colonial rule has been achieved, "divide-and-become free" has usually been amended to "divide-and-develop." The leaders of pre-industrial states face two inescapable facts of life. The first—well documented in innumerable reports and conferences of the United Nations—is that truly rapid development is impossible without substantial assistance from more industrialized societies. The second, although equally obvious, is one of those great secrets that everyone knows but nobody is supposed to talk about openly: the great powers seem more inclined to provide large amounts of development assistance without strings only when they believe they are offsetting the influence of a rival power. Thus, not only in Africa but throughout Asia and the Middle East, shrewd nationalist leaders have won substantial increments of assistance (and room for more autonomous maneuvering) by playing the Russians against the Americans and the Americans against the Russians. To a lesser degree this has meant promoting rivalry in financial and technical aid projects among the Western European nations also and even among some of the Eastern European nations. In the international gamesmanship of planning, as Burke notes, "the development plan and budget become a ploy in the game" (p. 58). Indeed, to understand the cold and austere language of a typical development plan or budget one must penetrate beyond the document and untangle the international web of bargaining with a large variety of governments, international agencies, consortia, and private corporations.

By the time Tanganyika won its independence the "bipolar balance of power" was already beginning to change. "Polycentrism" began to be felt in the communist world. Divisions appeared in the West, with De Gaulle challenging American influence in Europe. The Test Ban Treaty initiated a slow cooling off in the cold war and the beginnings of a _detente_ between the United States and the Soviet Union. From the viewpoint of their interest in world peace, the African leaders rejoiced at these developments and, indeed, contributed to them.

From the viewpoint of their economic development plans, however, many Africans were seriously upset. During a visit to a U.N. Africa seminar in Kampala, Uganda, in the spring of 1964 I had a chance to talk informally with intellectuals from many African countries. "If the cold war dies out," many of them asked, "how will your government succeed in getting Congressional approval for African aid funds?" But even at the time the question was being asked, the fears felt by my interrogators were being allayed by the emergence of a new Triad at the center of the world's power constellation. The Chinese were already mounting a world-wide drive against both the Russians and the Americans. If the conflict between the Russians and Americans seemed to abate, new and emotionally charged conflicts developed on the other legs of the triangle: between the Chinese and the Russians and the Chinese and the Americans. This situation has provided once again an opportunity for weak countries to become stronger by continuing their policy of divide-and-develop. This opportunity has been particularly conspicuous in East Africa, where the Chinese seem to have been concentrating their efforts. Indeed, at the time I was in Dar es Salaam, a Chinese mission was there to negotiate trade and aid agreements. The obvious Tanzanian desire to reach some quick agreements was, in my judgment, hardly unrelated to their potential effect on relations with Western countries.

FROM DIVIDE-AND-DEVELOP TO UNITE-AND-DEVELOP?

Can this "playing with fire" lead to Chinese control? It is highly unlikely. The very multiplicity of aid-giving countries militates against too much influence by any of them. More important, events in many countries, particularly in East Africa, "clearly demonstrate the refusal of African leaders to be regarded as inferior or as a ploy in a game not of their own making." [3] When China's Premier Chou En-lai visited Africa in 1965 he was rebuffed in many countries. When he offered aid, he was repeatedly outbid at once by the Russians. In Kenya, Zambia, and Burundi, vigorous action has been taken against local politicians who accepted Chi-

[3] Fred G. Burke, *Africa's Quest for World Order* (Englewood Cliffs, N.J.: Prentice-Hall, 1964), p. 150.

nese bribes. In Tanzania, where he was given a public reception, Tanzanian leaders publicly proclaimed, "We will not let anyone interfere in our internal policies." [4] Indeed, the very birth of Tanzania in 1964—as a union between Tanganyika and Zanzibar —is regarded by some as a farsighted African step to prevent Zanzibar from becoming a beachhead for Chinese or other communist penetration of East Africa.

Any foreign power operating in a developing country may, under certain conditions, try to serve its own interests by contributing to the peaceful or forcible overthrow of the host government. This is why divide-and-develop means playing with fire. Nevertheless, in certain circumstances the logic of divide-and-develop may lead to cooling, rather than fanning, the fires of international conflict. The donor country is inevitably interested in propaganda on its own behalf. But the most successful propaganda is the *propaganda of the deed*. Aid projects must be at least partially successful. No amount of publicity or speechmaking can cover up a downright failure. Thus, in the field of foreign aid American, Russian, and Chinese groups, with their allies from other countries, are inevitably engaged in peaceful competition. No matter how virulent the words of the Chinese may be, their actions involve them in competitive coexistence. What is more, the logic of competition— as has so often been proved true in ordinary markets—often leads to various forms of cooperation. An interesting case is provided by Afghanistan, where the Afghans have successfully played Americans against Russians to obtain more aid and better terms from both. In order to use this aid properly, the Afghans sought technical assistance in development planning. "In 1962, there were four teams of experts from aid-giving agencies in the Ministry of Planning—a five person team of Russians; a four person group of Americans . . . ; a group of five economists from West Germany; and a senior economic adviser with one assistant from the United Nations. The Ministry of Planning has been successful in bringing these experts with different backgrounds to a round table to discuss mutual problems. This approach is quite successful because it eliminates misunderstandings on the part of different aid-giving parties and creates a sense of cooperation among them and

---

[4] George de Carvalho, "Chou Runs Out of Hosts," Special Report, Africa *Life Magazine*, July 9, 1965, pp. 11–14.

the Afghans." [5] Thus, "divide-and-develop" may be subtly, almost imperceptibly, transformed into "unite-and-develop."

The forms of unified or cooperative action are many and diffuse. They may range from mere toleration to parallel action to exchange of information to stand-offish bargaining and partial collaboration. The successful development of a railroad, for example, cannot possibly be isolated from a host of other major factors in a country. Thus, at the request of both Tanzania and Zambia, a Chinese team of hydrological and geological experts have already initiated a study of a new railroad to give land-locked Zambia an economic lifeline to Dar es Salaam.[6] To pursue this project successfully—even in its earliest stages—the Chinese must consult with many people from other countries, particularly from the West. If they should carry it still further, they will have to cooperate with all the many kinds of people needed to build a railroad and operate it economically: contractors, shippers, farmers, agricultural advisers, mining experts, private and government enterprises, and a host of foreign experts, even including the "revisionist" Yugoslavs. Failure to win cooperation would mean failure for the Chinese—and "losing face" in Africa. This will be a fascinating operation to watch.

THE CONCENTRIC CIRCLES AND THE TRIAD

In watching the shifting conflict-cooperation relations among the big powers operating in countries like Tanzania, we need a broad perspective on the changing world patterns of power distribution. Otherwise we might easily expect too much too soon from the leaders of developing nations. We might too easily blame them for fomenting great-power disputes that have their basic ori-

[5] Azizullah Khogyanai, "Foreign Public Aid in National Planning" (unpublished seminar paper, Maxwell School, Syracuse University, 1964).

[6] Lawrence Fellows, "Chinese Communist in Tanzania For Survey of a New Rail Link," *New York Times,* August 24, 1965. The railway is regarded as "an uneconomic venture" by the International Bank for Reconstruction and Development, according to this same report. On the other hand, "Mr. Nyerere and President Kenneth D. Kaunda of Zambia are committed to building the railway whatever the difficulty in getting it financed. . . . Zambians feel that their present dependence on lifelines through Rhodesia, South Africa and the Portuguese territory of Mozambique makes them hostages to these governments, which are dominated by whites."

gins in the dynamics and pressures of large-scale industrialization. At the other extreme, one might easily exaggerate the international implications of any peaceful coexistence that the Tanzanians may be able to achieve among the Chinese, East Europeans, and Westerners assisting them in economic development.

The essence of such a broad perspective is to realize that countries like Tanzania, Kenya, and Uganda are in the Outermost Circles of the world power constellation. A single vote in the United Nations—although legally equal to that of any other country—is not directly related to its influence in world affairs, or even in the United Nations. Even when considered all together, the smaller nations of the world do not have anywhere near the economic power, military power, population, or moral power (which in this era flows partly from population size) of the Intermediate Circle. This is composed of such former great powers as Britain, France, Italy, West Germany, and Japan and such new forces as India, Pakistan, Indonesia, and Brazil. The disparity becomes still greater when we compare them with the Triad itself: the United States, the Soviet Union, and the Chinese People's Republic. Whether one likes it or not, it is in the Triad and the Intermediate Circle that we find the greatest potentials for eliminating the world's poverty through economic development or the world's population through a nuclear holocaust. The hope of economic development depends upon peaceful competition among the great powers. The hope of avoiding nuclear destruction depends upon accommodation and *detente,* particularly among the Big Three.

Nevertheless, the small countries have a role in promoting the competitive accommodation needed at the center of world power. This role is abrogated when a small country becomes a passive satellite in the shadow of one great power. It is perverted when a country tries to promote military conflict among the great powers in order to serve its own nationalist interests. Although this is not the place to call the "dishonor roll," such things have happened in recent years.

There have also been examples of small countries playing this role in a highly constructive manner. Many small countries in Africa and elsewhere displayed brilliant leadership in pushing toward the Test Ban Treaty. Many are revealing similar qualities in the current negotiations on the extension of the treaty and the prevention of "nuclear spread." In the more purely economic sphere important steps have been taken in the formation of the United Nations Trade and Assistance Board. Through this new organization the developing nations have challenged the industrialized nations to face up to the fact that their trade policies have tended to undermine their aid programs. On an individual basis, many small nations—Tanzania among them—are trying to build the economic basis for greater political independence by developing aid-trade relations with competing great powers. This strategy, of course, is bound to provoke temporary discomfort among great-power policy-makers, in the United States as much as anywhere else. This discomfort may manifest itself at times in anguished protests—or even threats of reprisal. Yet behind the discomfort, I suspect, there often lurks a growing awareness of the legitimacy of the strategy and a growing hope that it may be successful.

NATIONAL VS. TRANSNATIONAL SYSTEM-BUILDING

A major thrust of Burke's analysis is provided by his sharp distinction between "state" and "nation." Although Tanzania is a "state" possessing legal sovereignty, it "is not yet a nation, for it does not possess a sense of collective being or identity." Hence, when discussing most new African states, it may be misleading to use such terms as "new nations," "national planning," and "nationalism." In short, "what is currently under way in Tanzania may precisely be termed 'nation-building'; its development plan may be regarded as state planning for the purposes of constructing a 'nation'" (pp. 42–43).

For the economists, engineers, agronomists, and other specialists working on the specific parts of a development plan, planning is a technical process. It is something that would be undermined if narrow political considerations should become determining factors. Yet in a broader sense planning as a whole is a supremely political process, particularly when directed toward nation-building. "In a new nation like Tanzania," writes Dr. Anthony Rweyemamu, "a national plan is a major, albeit incomplete, substitute for the goods that were promised explicitly or implicitly during the struggle for independence. Insofar as it is indicative of a future of abundance, a national plan serves as a unifying agent of an otherwise loose and fragile society. . . . Therefore, even if the economic and social goals are not completely realized, a plan is successful to the extent to which it serves to mobilize the people's energies, bring about national integration and a measure of political consensus." [7] Thus, President Nyerere has called his first Five Year Plan a declaration of war calling upon everyone in the nation to be a soldier: "Our weapons are our hands and brains; on the land, in the factories, in the classroom, in hospitals; all of us, politicians, civil servants, soldiers, policemen, men, women and children. Let us say: 'It can be done; play your part.' " [8]

The political function of helping to integrate 125 tribal groupings into a nation is not something separable from the *economic* content of the plan. It is the economic specifics—better education, better health facilities, roads, new villages, aid to agriculture, new factories—that provide what Amitai Etzioni has called the "utilitarian power" in the hands of nation-building elites. These small specifics, when brought together into a properly legitimated plan, also provide "identitive power"; that is, unifying symbols of common aspiration. As Etzioni suggests in a fruitful set of hypotheses concerning political unification, the more utilitarian power and identification power the elites guiding unification command or build up, the more successful unification will be. These two forms of power may substantially reduce the need for using a third form, "coercive power," or force.[9] The three forms together, whatever their relative share of emphasis, are all needed to weave the complex web of internal relations that comprise a national system.

Yet "the key to successful nation-building for Tanzania" as Burke points out, also lies "at the suprastate level." In part, this means maintaining its position in the loose but extremely advantageous transnational system represented by the Sterling Area and Commonwealth preference. Any eventual British membership in the European Common Market would upset the existing Common-

[7] *Nation-Building and the Planning Processes in Tanzania*, pp. 95, 241.

[8] *Ibid.*, p. 94.

[9] *Political Unification* (New York: Holt, Rinehart and Winston, 1965), pp. 71–73, 94. Although this book deals mainly with the unification of previously existing nations, much of the analysis "also serves the study of the formation of a nation out of tribes, villages, or feudal fiefs or the merger of two suburbs, corporations, or ethnic groups" (p. xviii).

wealth system and challenge Tanzania's viability (p. 74). In much larger part, the key to significant progress under Tanzanian development planning lies in steps toward integrating the economies of the East African countries: Kenya, Uganda, and Tanzania. Separately, each of these countries is too small to provide the markets and resource base needed for rapid development or for healthy adjustment to changes in the world market structure. This is why "in 1960 Dr. Nyerere indicated he even was willing to postpone the date for Tanganyika's independence if this could help the formation of an East African Federation" (p. 91).

Once the East African states achieved independence, however, the great dream of federation began to look less attractive and less feasible. The common market arrangements began to weaken. Under pressure from Tanzania, the "Kampala agreement" was negotiated in May 1965 in the hope of achieving a mutually acceptable allocation of new manufacturing plants among the three countries.[10] It is now widely referred to as the "Kampala disagreement." Tanzania has already announced her intention to break away from the East African Currency board and establish its own national currency. With these significant reductions in the system of economic integration inherited from the British, it is not surprising that serious moves toward full political federation—apart from ritualistic obeisance to the ideal of federation—have been suspended.

One can find many factors that help explain this withdrawal from a transnational system. For one thing, the transnational East African system was primarily a British achievement. It was developed by the British first as an economical basis for consolidating colonial rule and then as a contribution toward British disengagement. It reflected the interests of British expatriates and settlers in East Africa, particularly the large nucleus of white settlers in Kenya. What could be more natural—and indeed essential—than that the Africans should now examine this legacy carefully and adjust it to meet their own needs as *they* see them? Moreover, there is no doubt that the inherited arrangements tended to favor the most developed country, Kenya, and discriminate against the least

[10] Rweyemamu, *Nation-Building and the Planning Processes in Tanzania,* pp. 70–78.

developed one, Tanzania: hence, the Kampala agreement, the dis-
agreements stemming from it, and the succession of new agreements that are bound to come in the future . . .

In a more fundamental sense, however, there is an inherent
conflict between simultaneous building of a national and a transnational system. The two efforts compete for the time and energy
of a small minority of leaders and for the meager resources at their
disposal. If state planning to construct a nation may be likened
to the conduct of a war, an effort to build a transnational system
at the same time would be like conducting a war on two fronts. It
could mean defeat on both. Indeed, one might even offer the hy-
pothesis that peaceful transnational federation is possible only if
the units that federate are really nations. Students of small groups
and organizations long ago learned that individuals cannot become
responsible members of a larger entity unless they can first develop a sense of self and personal identity. Ego maturation—despite the disturbances it leads to during puberty and adolescence—
is a prerequisite of interpersonal cooperation. In the same sense,
nation-building and nationalism may be seen as a prerequisite of
international cooperation. Although it may lead in some cases to
"totalistic" or aggressive nationalism,[11] it also provides the building blocks for subsequent transnational groupings and produces
more mature actors in an emerging world society.

ONE-PARTY SYSTEMS AND DEMOCRATIC MYTHS

The Western model of political democracy is one of the great
ideals and triumphs of modern industrialism. By allowing freedom
of political organization and offering voters a choice among candidates of opposing parties, it provides a valuable check upon the
power of dominant groups. It provides invaluable opportunities for
the expression of submerged interests and the rise of new and more
creative leaders.

Yet when a competitive party system is regarded as the essence
and touchstone of democracy in Western societies, the model de-
generates. It becomes a way of ignoring the vast—and to some

---

[11] Robin Williams, *American Society* (New York: Knopf, 1960), pp. 456–60.
Although this discussion of nationalism concentrates upon America, Williams'
distinction between "totalistic" and "pluralistic" nationalism is internationally
applicable.

extent irreversible—shift of significant decision-making from the
vague generalities of political campaigns to the daily activities of
executive agencies. It has little bearing upon the detailed processes
of technical research and of ceaseless bargaining among and within
the vast bureaucracies of government agencies, corporations, and
organized interest groups. Nor will far-reaching action to remedy
the many defects in any competitive party system necessarily lead
to an extension of genuine democracy throughout a society. To
provide for more widespread and significant participation in society, a country needs not only political democracy but also:

> —*individual democracy,* which provides individuals with the
> rights of juridical self-defense;
> —*economic democracy,* which provides full opportunities for
> useful employment and for at least minimum standards of
> food, shelter, clothing, medical care, education, and recrea-
> tion;
> —*social democracy,* which provides guarantees that political
> and economic rights shall not be impaired because of a per-
> son's color, race, religion, national origin, or sex; and
> —*organizational democracy,* which provides the members of
> organizations with challenging work, offers opportunities for
> individualism and self-development, and recognizes individual
> rights and responsibilities.

Any significant effort to evaluate or improve democratic institutions in any country requires attention to *all* of these forms of
democracy.[12]

The traditional democratic model becomes a dangerous myth
when automatically applied—as has so often been done by Western political leaders—to pre-industrial, developing societies. At
best, it becomes a way of proclaiming the superiority of Westerners
and the inferiority of new states. At worst, it confuses outward
form with underlying reality. It obscures the real-life choices available to the nation-builders. It prevents any real understanding of
what is happening in many new states in which a dominant mass
party such as Tanzania's TANU is "the major instrument in nation-

---

[12] Bertram M. Gross, "The Five Pillars of Democracy," in *The Managing
of Organizations* (New York: Free Press, 1964), pp. 830–31.

building" (p. 46). It may even lead to breaches in economic or political relations—as when aid or recognition is suspended on the ground that a one-party political system violates democratic principles. Although this reason is usually a rationalization of action taken on other grounds also, it is unquestionably a factor in the tangled skein of international politics.

Tanzania's President, Julius Nyerere, has replied vigorously to Western criticism of the one-party monopoly enjoyed by TANU. He has not only attacked the idea that the two-party system is equivalent to democracy. He has also attacked the statement—often expressed by Westerners—that "the conditions for democracy do not really exist in such and such a country." His rebuttal: "What is really meant is that the conditions for a two-party system do not exist; the only place of which it would be reasonable to say that the conditions for democracy did not exist would be an uninhabited island—or a lunatic asylum! For the 'conditions' of democracy (or for self-government, which is the same thing) exist wherever man exists as a rational human being." Maintaining that "democracy, in the true sense, is as familiar to the Africans as the tropical sun," he points to the traditional decision-making method in a typical African village: "The Elders sit under the big tree, and talk until they agree." He points to the intraparty democracy within TANU, including the intraparty disputes that are brought into the open in Parliament. Above all, he strongly suggests that under the conditions existing in his country, competitive parties would lead to a dissolution of the State.[13]

Considerable support for a large part of Nyerere's position is provided by an American political scientist, Milton Esman, who has analyzed the relation of party systems to development processes in pre-industrial societies. Esman has distinguished five types of party systems: (1) conservative oligarchies (Iran, Ethiopia, Northern Nigeria, Afghanistan, and Peru); (2) competitive interest-oriented parties (Philippines, Brazil, Greece, Chile, Malaya, and Jamaica); (3) authoritarian military reformers (Pakistan, Burma, South Korea, Thailand, and the Sudan); (4) dominant mass parties (Mexico, India, Egypt, Algeria, Puerto Rico, Tanzania, Tunisia, and Guinea); and (5) communist totalitarians (China,

---

[13] Julius K. Nyerere, "Democracy and the Party System" (Dar es Salaam: Tanganyika Standard Limited, 1963).

Soviet Union, and the communist countries of Eastern Europe). "The dominant mass party regimes," he finds, "appear to combine the advantages of purposeful leadership, a developmentally oriented doctrine, the capacity both to mobilize and to discipline widespread support and participation, and the ability to deploy a variety of action and communication instruments. For these reasons, this type of regime seems to be particularly relevant to the needs of transitional societies undergoing rapid and radical transformation." [14]

In the light of Esman's analysis, one might well speculate that in Tanzania, as in many similar societies, the only viable alternative to a dominant mass party may be a conservative oligarchy or an authoritarian military junta.

President Nyerere's case for the possibilities of genuine intraparty democracy in a one-party system was strengthened by TANU's new 1965 constitution. Among many other changes, the new constitution provided for the possibility of opposing party candidates in primary contests.[15] This new system was tried out in the national elections of September 1965. Under the headline "It Worked," the British *Economist* provided the following commentary on these elections:

> The Tanzanians responded to their opportunities with gusto: They flung out nine ministers, two of them senior ministers. . . . The importance to Tanzania of these elections is considerable. The results went some way to vindicate President Nyerere's claim that his one-party state has elements of democracy in it (but if he uses his power to nominate ten members of parliament as a means of putting all his sacked ministers back the impression will be spoiled). He himself got an overwhelming personal vote—no less in the island of Zanzibar than on the mainland; the tenuous unity between Tanzania's two parts is the stronger for it. And a white minister, Mr. Derek Bryceson, was overwhelmingly re-elected by his dark constituents.[16]

[14] Milton Esman, "The Politics of Development Administration," Occasional Paper, Comparative Administration Group, American Society for Public Administration, 1963.

[15] Rweyemamu, *Nation-Building and the Planning Processes in Tanzania*, pp. 262–67.

[16] October 2, 1963, p. 24.

SHATTERED DREAMS ON THE PATHS OF PROGRESS

After years of typically colonial inactivity in East Africa, the British finally came up with a gigantic plan to help meet Britain's postwar needs for protein and margarine by large-scale agricultural development in East Africa, mainly Tanganyika. "With un-British boldness and audacity which we might charge to war fatigue or boredom, they called for clearing not thousands but three million acres of tsetse-infested, relatively uninhabited land and the subsequent planting of this virgin soil with groundnuts" (p. 34). In "Peanuts, the Things of Which Dreams Are Fashioned" Burke depicts the tragic shattering of this plan.

There are many lessons that may be drawn from the record of this failure. One is the presumed futility of all large-scale planning by government agencies. Indeed, for opponents of government planning, the story of the groundnut scheme is a favorite text. The lesson drawn by Burke is more sophisticated. The failure of the plan, Burke suggests, was due partly to the lack of on-the-ground studies and pilot operations with respect to rainfall, soil, logistics, and the suitability of earthmoving equipment designed for use in other environments, and partly to the nonparticipation of East Africans familiar with local conditions. The significance of this lesson does not lie in what might be learned by the handful of colonial governments still remaining; the only important lesson for them to learn is the danger to themselves and the world inherent in their efforts to continue colonial rule. The lesson is significant, rather, for the development planners of new states. In their own way, they can too easily repeat the errors of their imperial predecessors. Indeed, throughout the developing countries of Africa, Asia, the Middle East, and Latin America there are scores upon scores of "white elephants"—ambitious projects which, like the groundnut scheme, were launched without adequate technical preparation or local participation.

Indeed, for a while it almost seemed that Tanzania's "villagization" program would become such a white elephant. At first, plans were made for a small "series of 'pilot' settlement projects to serve as experimental stations for future development" (p. 73). By 1964, on a sudden wave of enthusiasm, this modest program was expanded into a vast plan for transforming the countryside. It became

—in Dr. Rweyemamu's words—"a massive dynamic program seeking rapid and far-reaching modernization through a relocation of hundreds of thousands of peoples into compact agricultural villages. The program is intended to be revolutionary in its impact insofar as it aims at drastic alteration of customs, ways of life and attitudes of rural peoples, thereby fashioning a new political society." [17] For a while it seemed that ambitious dreams might lead to a serious wastage of resources through precipitate and ill-considered settlement projects. But the difficulties of on-the-ground implementation forced more careful action. The latest indications are that the program will be returned to its original form as a series of pilot projects.

And yet there is another—and far more subtle—lesson that may be gleaned from the groundnut experience. "The smashed hopes, partially cleared land, machinery and rights to land were eventually turned over to the Tanganyika Agricultural Corporation (TAC)," which initiated a program of farm settlements. Subsequently, TAC was abolished; its assets were turned over to the Tanganyika Development Corporation, one of the major new forces in promoting commercial and industrial projects in Tanganyika.[18] But by the time the new villagization program got under way, it became evident that a major source of strength was to be found: a number of the settlement projects started by TAC. These by-products of British failure are now incorporated in—and contributing to—the ongoing program of the Tanzanians. In addition, the British failure left Tanzania with such legacies as a new port, a new rail line, and the knowledge and skills painfully acquired by both natives and expatriates involved in the project. Thus, when we point out that a plan may have unforeseeable consequences, we must keep two kinds of consequences in mind. We must not focus entirely on the possibility that an auspicious beginning may be followed by dire consequences. We must also bear in mind the possibility that immediate failures may lead to subsequent gains.

Nor should the failure of one ambitious project lead to a stifling of imagination and a cautious avoidance of risky ventures. The history of successful industrial development in the Western na-

[17] *Nation-Building and the Planning Process in Tanzania,* p. 137.
[18] *Ibid.,* p. 122.

tions is, in large part, a history of great risks—and great failures. "Trailblazing is a risky affair. Hundreds of the industrial pioneers in the late nineteenth and early twentieth century went bankrupt in the effort. The wreckage of the first automobile companies was part of the process that led to the General Motors Corporation and the other 'immortals' that now bestride the automobile industry in the U.S.A. In this case some of the earlier companies rose from the grave of bankruptcy and through merger or consolidation returned again to the heights of administrative power." [19] In their drive for accelerated development in the last third of the twentieth century, the leaders of "developing nations" can hardly afford to be paralyzed by the overcautious fear of failure. They must heed the warning in the Book of Proverbs: "Where there is no vision, the people perish." They could well instruct their technicians to ponder the words of the prophet Joel: "Your old men shall dream dreams, your young men shall see visions." Without visions and dreams there can be no meaningful planning for the building of a nation, for the growth of its economy or for the happiness of its people. The danger of futile utopianism does not lie in the grandeur of a vision or the beauty of a dream. It lies rather in the failure to concentrate on the myriad details of today and tomorrow (for this

[19] Gross, *The Managing of Organizations*, p. 665. In the private-enterprise sector, failures are not as much of a public spectacle as with governmental failures, nor need they—except in time of depression—have serious political repercussions. This is one of the reasons why governmental planners are often well advised to have a significant burden of developmental responsibility, where feasible, assumed by private enterprise. Whether the probability of failure is greater or lesser under private sponsorship is not something that can be assayed in abstract terms apart from the specific circumstances. In any case one is tempted to speculate on what the outcome of the British groundnut plan might have been if the Unilever subsidiary which originated the idea (Burke, p. 34) had carried it out by itself instead of turning it over to the British government.

[20] Note the contrary view expressed by Wassily Leontief, the developer of modern input-output analysis: "Planning is the organized application of systematic reasoning to the solution of specific practical problems. An alternative to planning is the trial and error method. . . . A trial and error procedure can be considered successful whenever over a reasonably long run of trials the combined gains exceed by a healthy margin the total losses." ("The Anatomy of Planning," address before the Canadian Manufacturers' Association, Toronto, June 3, 1963). Yet a sober review of work in input-output analysis would probably indicate a considerable use of trial and error methods. In fact, learning by trial and error is so fundamental in econometrics that it has been given a special label: the method of successive approximations.

is where the future is made) and the failure to learn today from yesterday's errors. Despite the claims sometimes made on its behalf, whether at the national level or that of a single organization, sound planning is no substitute for trial and error.[20] It is rather an organized effort at "intended" rationality and continuous learning on the basis of experience.

BERTRAM M. GROSS

Syracuse, New York
Fall 1965

I

The Setting for Planning

On December 9, 1961, in a ceremony that would have done justice
to Ernest Hemingway, a new green, gold, and black flag was raised
atop snow-covered Mt. Kilimanjaro, and in Dar es Salaam, Dr.
Julius Nyerere, the first prime minister of an independent Tanganyika, accepted the transfer of authority from the British, who
forty-one years earlier had been charged by the League of Nations
with the administration of the near-bankrupt former German
colony.

Tanganyika, covering an area of nearly 363,000 square miles
in East Africa, is bounded by Lakes Victoria, Tanganyika, and
Malawi, and the Indian Ocean. The greater part of the country
consists of an enormous plateau reaching more than 600 miles from
Lake Tanganyika in the west nearly to the Indian Ocean in the
east.

Geographically the country tends to fall into three regions, or
zones. The coastal lowlands enjoy an annual rainfall of forty to
fifty inches with a distinct hot season from December to March.
The central plateau region, with an average altitude exceeding four
thousand feet, is sharply defined along its eastern and western mar-
gins by steep escarpments, in some places reaching heights greater
than seven thousand feet. Rainfall in the plateau region varies from
place to place and from year to year but averages about thirty
inches. The last major zone in this extraordinarily varied country
is the highland region in the vicinity of the lakes and the Great Rift
Valley. Also included in this region are the mountain areas of the
Northern Province. This fertile lake and mountain region is the

1

most heavily populated part of the country. There are, for example, more than 600,000 people living on the slopes of Mt. Kilimanjaro alone.

The natural increase of the African population varies from
region to region but is believed to be remarkably low, somewhere
in the vicinity of 2.2 per cent a year. People of Asian origin—nearly
all from the Indian subcontinent—making up slightly less than 1
per cent of the population are increasing at about 2.5 per cent.
Over-all population density, though varying enormously from region
to region, averages twenty-six per square mile.

TABLE 1

POPULATION (IN THOUSANDS) BY RACIAL COMPOSITION

	1957 Census	1961 Estimate	1962 Estimate
Africans	8,637.0	9,419.0	9,560.0
Europeans	20.7	22.3	21.4
Indians & Pakistanis	77.6	87.3	87.3
Arabs	19.7	27.8	26.8
Goans & Others	3.9	4.9	4.8
Total	8,758.9	9,561.3	9,700.3

Source: Tanganyika Statistical Abstract, 1962, p. 11.

HISTORICAL PERSPECTIVES

Men of various hues and cultures have planned and schemed
for the future of this vast territory now termed Tanzania. Two
thousand years before Columbus sailed the Atlantic, Greek and
Arab merchants contested for the trade along the Tanganyika coast.
Ten years after Columbus discovered the Americas, Vasco da
Gama weighed anchor at Kilwa. However, it was the Arabs who
dominated the coast until the latter half of the nineteenth century.
The Sultan of Oman, Said Den, for example, in the early half of
the nineteenth century planned to establish an elaborate trading
system with the people of the interior of Tanganyika. His merchants ranged far inland, returning to the coast with slaves and
ivory which they exchanged for the produce of the Orient. The
Handbook of Tanganyika reveals that "in 1828 an American mer-
chant named Edmond Roberts reported that he had frequently
seen Zanzibar elephant hunters whose homes were a thirty days

march away in the interior, and that the government of Zanzibar occasionally sent presents to the negro kings a long distance inland." [1]

The area formerly known as Tanganyika first attracted the attention of Europeans through the exploits of the early traveler-explorers such as Krapf, Rebmann, Burton, Speke, and, most important of all, Livingstone. The Sultan of Zanzibar possessed an ill-defined suzerainty over the hinterland of the East African littoral which Great Britain was committed to support in exchange for the Sultan's agreement to abolish the slave trade. However, the subsequent scramble for Africa introduced a new element of competition between the European powers; and while Egypt, France, and Britain competed for the favor of the Kabaka Mutesa of Buganda, Karl Peters, the German explorer, was quietly carving out the vast area subsequently known as Tanganyika for Imperial Germany. The machinations of the European powers were such that by 1885 Great Britain found that she could no longer maintain the integrity of the Sultan's domains on the Tanganyika coast. That year, at Berlin, Great Britain and the other major European powers recognized Tanganyika as a German colony.

In the 1880's the German-Africa Society of Berlin and the German Colonization Society began to plan for the settlement of East Africa. The Imperial German government assumed control over the East African territories from the German East African Company in 1891 and almost immediately undertook to subjugate the rebellious tribes of the interior. In the process of establishing its rule over the tribes in the hinterlands, German forces effectively destroyed many of the traditional tribal sociopolitical systems. Although a variety of schemes were put forth by the German Colonial government to develop the new territory, a series of bloody and costly uprisings consumed the greater part of available resources and by the time of the First World War left much of the country despoiled and depopulated.[2] However, in certain areas of developmental planning the Germans excelled even in this early period. For example, in 1911 the German Colonial Institute reported that there were more than 1,000 schools and nearly 6,700 students in the colony.[3] Growing of African cash crops, especially cotton, were encouraged and assisted, and sisal and rubber were early developed as European plantation industries. Exports by 1906 had reached about .5 million pounds in gross value and imports two years before the outbreak of the First World War exceeded 2.5 million pounds.

Although no historian recorded or publicized their schemes, we can safely assume that the Africans also formulated and sought to execute plans for the future of the lands later known as Tanganyika. The Wahehe, for example, under the leadership of their paramount chief Mkwawa in the latter part of the nineteenth century, were in the process of carrying out a military consolidation of much of the southeastern interior of this vast territory. Mkwawa's plans, however, conflicted with those of the German administration. Even though he successfully ambushed and nearly annihilated a German contingent of 250 soldiers in 1891, his army was finally defeated. The German commander dramatized the victory by sending Mkwawa's skull to Germany, where it eventually found its way to the Bremen Museum. Many years later, in 1954, Chief Adam Sapi, the grandson of Mkwawa and present speaker of the Tanganyika Parliament, presided at a ceremony commemorating the return of his grandfather's skull to the land of the Wahehe and its enshrinement in an elaborate mausoleum. Thus, development and planning for the land and the people of Hehe, for the seventy years after the ambush, were initiated first by Germans and after 1921 by the British. This is not to say, however, that the Wahehe, and other peoples of Tanganyika, even during this period of external rule, were completely without plans for their own future.

PLANNING: AN OVERVIEW

The term "planning" is employed in a variety of ways by different peoples for various purposes. For this preliminary survey of the background to planning in Tanganyika, the "national plan," in its broadest sense, is a description of *a desirable state of affairs projected to a given point in the future, supported by an outline of the steps thought requisite to achieve that state.* The "plan," by postulating a desirable state of affairs, provides its exponents with a public cause capable of furthering the legitimacy of their rule, as well as posing a constant challenge to them to produce the state of affairs implicit in the plan.

The major significance of this preliminary survey does not rest in new data that it might uncover but rather in the extent to which the process of postulating, projecting, and then moving toward a certain state of affairs in a new African country gives rise to some new insights into the general nature of this uniquely human process. Although it is not possible to do so, it might eventually be desirable to approach a major study of "planning" in Tanganyika by first regarding the land mass and peoples of the territory as a "situation" that various men and nations have sought to alter in order to bring the country closer to the model they have implicitly or explicitly formulated. Various factors through time have served to further certain plans and frustrate others. The land and peoples of Tanganyika are in part the product of earlier visions and plans, and their capacity to realize a future state of well-being is in part dependent on the nature of the plans men have already worked out in this vast land and for this complex people over the past three centuries. But such "ambitious plans" of our own must await another day. The present survey will concentrate upon the more recent past and deal almost wholly with the three stages of planning that have occurred since the advent of British hegemony in 1921.

A major initial observation that emerges from even a preliminary study of planning in Tanganyika—which prior to its independence in 1961 had never known any state but one of dependence on external economies and polities—is that national planning, in the proper sense of the term, has never existed. The suspicion that national planning, even in the highly developed nations, is nowadays inconsistent with trends toward economic interdependency and new, more inclusive political associations, gains added impact when viewed with reference to the newly emergent territories of Africa. Design and initiation of the first stage of planning for Tanganyika, with which we are concerned, cannot be found in Tanganyika but rather must be inferred from British colonial policy of that period. The details of colonial policy, as they imparted a transnational plan for a future state of affairs for Tanganyika, emerge only after we scrutinize the innumerable committee reports on colonial problems, colonial office and colonial government papers, and relevant statements made by colonial secretaries and governors.

However, if we are to assess accurately the impact of the key variables upon the planning process in a colonial situation and upon policy execution, it behooves us to weigh the influence of political events and economic thinking in Great Britain; for until December 1961 the image of what Tanganyika should be was shaped not in Dar es Salaam but in London and was molded according to the over-all dictates of colonial policy, the cold war, and the influence of the Trusteeship Council of the United Nations. However, it would be misleading to imply that the major forces that have determined the image or model of the Tanganyika-to-be are highly structured or predictable in all of their elements. For one of the more fascinating, but at the same time frustrating, aspects of this process is the highly unstructured, variable, and unpredictable role played by unique individuals and extraordinary events. Colonial governors and administrators through the years, despite general policy direction from the Colonial Office and the United Nations, have stamped the imprint of their personal "plan" in bold colors upon the land and peoples of Tanganyika. The Colonial governments, led by the governor, have possessed remarkable independence and have so intimately identified themselves with the territory as to reshape general colonial plans in order to further the interests or future of Tanganyika according to their own minds.

Before facing the question of whose interests the various decision-makers who have schemed and planned over this great land sought to further, it is necessary to digress somewhat and note another aspect of the current state of man's political realm.

PLANNING AND THE NATURE OF AUTHORITY

Everywhere today men support the myth that a nation's leaders rule and plan in the name and interests of the "people." Possibly the most profound political consequence of the Second World War, and at the same time an extraordinary testimony to the pervasiveness in our era of the ideology of equality and majority rule, is the universal requirement that demands that all rulers exercise authority in the name of the "people." Deference to the will of the gods or their high priests, to the state, or to one's ancestors no longer legitimizes the rule of the few over the many. Popular sovereignty, even though not everywhere expressed in terms of universal suffrage, has emerged as a sole justification for the making and enforcing of authoritative decisions. This extraordinary phenomenon is not without relevance to "planning," for it dictates that the future state of affairs, postulated in a plan, must obtain the support of the "people"; that those who do plan must take into account the expectations of the "people" as to what the nation ought to be like five, ten, or fifteen years hence. What is significant here is not so much whether the plan of the decision-makers accurately reflects the expectations of the "people," for it is apparent to all that in much of the world today public consent is rarely sought. What is important is the universality of the myth of popular sovereignty, for it in turn gives rise to two additional tendencies that directly affect the planning process.

So long as men ruled other men and planned their collective and individual futures by the grace of God or the will of the ancestors, it was not necessary for the plans to be public property or even public knowledge. More important is the fact that success, and thus tenure as a leader in a traditional political system, did not depend upon the extent to which the elite's plans were fulfilled. Popular sovereignty, however, not only permits judgments of the efficacy of leadership but encourages competition for positions of leadership and competition between rival promises or "plans" as to what the future state of affairs ought to be or how the government should proceed to achieve that state of affairs. In this fashion, rival plans for the future of the nation bid against each other and there is a tendency for the bidding further to widen the gap between exaggerated expectation and the realistic capacity of any government to meet those expectations.

The second implication of popular sovereignty leadership for planning, viewed in this fashion, concerns the issue of democracy. To retain its leadership position, an existing elite is required to approximate the promises made by an opposition, promises it is not possible to keep. To meet this challenge to its leadership, the existing elite frequently finds it necessary either to eliminate or to neutralize the opposition so as to narrow the gap between the capacity of the government to produce and the expectations of the people as to what should be produced; or the existing elite might choose to manipulate the "people" into believing that government is in fact meeting their expectations as planned. Recent political events in Tanganyika, as are noted in more detail below, show clearly the extraordinary force of the interrelation of planning and popular sovereignty upon the political vitality and stability of a new nation.

Even in the early stages of British colonial rule in Tanganyika, there existed a sense of ruling not in the interests solely of Britain but in the interests of the "people." Here, of course, it is important to draw attention to the unique status of Tanganyika as a ward of the international community entrusted to the care of Great Britain. The plans of Englishmen for the future of Tanganyika, therefore, have had to take into account Article 22 of the Covenant of the League of Nations:

> To those colonies and territories which as a consequence of the late war have ceased to be under the sovereignty of the states which formerly governed them and which are inhabited by peoples not yet able to stand by themselves under the strenuous conditions of the modern world, there should be applied the principles that the well-being and development of such peoples form a sacred trust to civilization.

Thus, from its very inception planning for Tanganyika was an international enterprise. Though independent in the legal sense, planning in Tanganyika continues to be an international undertaking.

Plans for whom, in whose interests, and with whose consent changed gradually with the interests being initially defined by the British administrators with only slight deference to the opinion of the indigenous population. But as the role of the "people" of Tanganyika—first that of a small European minority and later the large African majority—grew in importance, the popular interest as reflected in planning statements of policy was redefined accordingly. One of the least understood but possibly most significant aspects of political transition in the new nations is this constant redefinition of the "popular will."

Those aspects of national planning in Tanganyika which it is thought might contribute to the formulation of some general propositions can best be identified by viewing the process in three chronological phases: the commencement of British rule in 1920 to the Second World War; the war and immediate postwar years; and the period from about 1945 to the present.

 II

Engagement—To Plan Is Not to Plan

British penetration and subsequent rule in East Africa, in good English fashion, was little planned and is thought by some to have happened in a fit of absent-mindedness. Although an earlier generation of Englishmen had planned, schemed, and dreamed of an African empire stretching from the Cape to Cairo, little planning went into the actual acquisition of Tanganyika and no plans existed or were rapidly forthcoming for its development. The territory after the First World War was in a dangerous state. According to the *Handbook of Tanganyika,* "the territory's economy, its communications and its inhabitants had been disrupted by the East African Campaign, and Tanganyika did not escape the influenza epidemic of 1917–19 which was estimated . . . to have caused between 50,000 and 80,000 deaths." [1] Famine, disease, and a breakdown in administration characterized the country in the postwar years. To cope with this task, the Colonial Office had fewer than 600 British civil servants in the country as of 1924.[2] There was little time or available personnel to do anything but attempt to re-establish, reorganize, re-equip, and rebuild. It was not until 1923/24 that the treasury, for example, was able to show even a slight surplus. In that year the economy finally reached the level it had obtained in 1913 under German rule.

MARKING TIME

Only the most visionary administrator or missionary in this early period thought or planned in terms of African self-government

9

and independence. The implicit plan was pragmatically to make the best of the existing situation. During this interwar period British imperial policy generally took the view that responsible government was not appropriate for Africans, but that if a European settler population existed in a colonial territory it was desirable to extend to that element gradually an increasing degree of self-government. This attitude was reflected first in the establishment of an executive council in 1920 comprising the governor, chief secretary, attorney general, treasurer, and principal medical officer. In 1924 the director of education and the secretary for native affairs were included in the Executive Council. More important, however, was the establishment in 1926 of a legislative council consisting of thirteen official and ten nonofficial members including three Asians. It was not until after the Second World War that Africans were nominated to the Legislative Council and not until 1957 that a ministerial system was introduced. Here we might also note that although members of the Executive Council have always sat in the Legislative Council, the direct and full responsibility of the Executive Council to the legislature was not achieved until the establishment of full representative government in 1960. Thus, the effective government of the territory, until very recently, has tended to rest with a governor, his advisers, and the heads of departments. Having said this, however, we must immediately draw attention to the extraordinary power and autonomy of the Provincial Administration with its unique control over the governance of the African population. The Provincial Administration was almost solely responsible for the development of native authorities. Thus, in one sense the earliest stage of development was of an administrative and political nature with an emphasis upon development at the lower levels. The attitude of the colonial administration toward the governance of the African population seemed to be that of doing only what was necessary to secure sufficient revenue to cover the cost of administration. In common with policy elsewhere in East Africa, the principle of indirect rule was applied and the territory was administered by a hierarchy of expatriate officers at the territorial, provincial, and district levels operating through a variety of types of African native authorities, some indigenous but most established simply for this purpose. There developed, as a consequence of this dual attitude and approach, a marked divergence between the law and order and the tax collection governance of the vast, widely scattered African population and the governance of the European-settler community.

The export economy, almost solely in the hands of European and Asian planters and businessmen, boomed during the latter half of the 1920's. For example, exports of sisal, the major cash crop, rose from about twenty-one thousand tons in 1913 to nearly forty-six thousand in 1929; coffee increased from about a thousand tons in 1913 to six thousand in 1925 and more than ten thousand in 1928. During the same period the rural road network begun by the Germans was extended, some new roads were surveyed and built, and government grants to mission schools were initiated. But this was done without reference to planning for Tanganyika per se. It rather reflected the amalgam of Colonial Office general policy, settler influence, and the initiative of individual administrators.

INDIRECT RULE AND LOCAL DEVELOPMENT

The emphasis upon indirect rule through native authorities in a country characterized by diffuse small-scale traditional governing systems is indicative of government's policy of maintaining the status quo by establishing a political system based upon parochial administration through native authorities.[3]

The meager resources allocated to improve education in this early period were designed to reinforce the status quo by training sons of the appointed chiefs so that indirect rule in the next generation would become institutionalized and correspondingly more effective. The significance of this emphasis upon developing a decentralized system of indirect rule by native authorities, in addition to the parochialism that it inevitably fostered, was the implied requirement that large-scale planning for a revised model of Tanganyika would inevitably require concentration on the local level where considerable investment in administrative capacity had already been made. Thus, one of the characteristics of development in many British territories, or former British territories, in contrast to former colonies of Belgium or France, has been the initiation and furtherance of "development from below." This emphasis not only set the tone for a uniquely British colonial policy of parochial paternalism but also determined the order of development priority and the subsequent scale of planning activities. A memo on native policy in East Africa in 1930 noted:

> It must be the aim of the administration of every territory with regard to all the inhabitants, irrespective of race or religion, to maintain order, to administer justice, to promote health and education, to provide means of communication and transport and generally to promote the industrial and commercial development of the country.[4]

CRISIS SITUATIONS AND PLANNING

Men rarely take the time or expend the energy required to make plans as to how to go about achieving an altered state of affairs unless there exists a relatively intense and timely dissatisfaction either with the existing state of affairs or with the steps that are currently being employed to reach an earlier postulated state of affairs. For example, it is possible to identify a spate of uncoordinated plans at the assumption of administrative control in Tanganyika by Great Britain in 1920 in response to the enormous task of rehabilitating the territory. Thus, in that year the director of education was required to prepare a report on establishing an educational system to train boys "suitable to the administrative needs of the territory and fit to take an active part in the economic development of the country." [5]

Signs of impending war in Europe in 1937 were partly responsible for the establishment of the first Central Development Committee in Tanganyika. The governor of Tanganyika in his budget speech of 1936 drew attention to the political uncertainty in East Africa and to the crisis situation which required that the government formulate plans to cope with the situation:

> One factor in the life of Tanganyika of which we have all been uneasily conscious during the present year is that of its political future. While it is unquestionable that the publicity given in Europe to doubts expressed upon this matter have a certain effect in checking the investment of capital in the country, it is easy to exaggerate the force of that effect by

disassociating it—as one cannot, I venture to suggest, legitimately do—from the general state of political uncertainty, created by the recent upheaval in Abyssinia, which is also, in a sense, a part of East Africa.[6]

It was in this mood that the first Central Development Committee was established with a view that it could restore confidence and establish machinery for development consistent with the apparent threat. Unfortunately, this initial explicit effort at planned development was short-lived. Eight months after it was inaugurated, when war broke out, it suspended its activities.

ADMINISTRATIVE ROADBLOCKS

During this early period, and even prior to the first attempts at planned development, it is possible to identify efforts to move in a certain direction by examining the annual budgets which were, in effect, the principal instruments for the control and development of the economy. The Colonial Government Budget has traditionally been compiled in the financial secretary's office on the basis of estimates submitted by departments and by the provincial administration. The provincial administration in turn derives its estimates from plans submitted by the constituent districts. It was the provincial administration that was ultimately responsible for evaluating the requests and requirements of the native authorities and district administrations. Although the financial secretary has always played an important part in determining the form and scope of the budget, the final decision rested with the governor and Executive Council.

The budget-drafting procedure required that the financial secretary project forecasts of revenue from anticipated tax returns. Since the primary source of revenue was customs duties, statistics concerning imports and exports have always been the most comprehensive. Other statistics that were compiled were usually less reliable and seldom used for fiscal projections. In fact, it was not until after the war that the national income accounts, industrial production schedules, and capital formation figures were employed in drafting the budget. The significance of the budget-drafting procedure is that until recently its primitive nature precluded extensive and sophisticated long-range planning and in the technical meaning of the term there was no "planning." So long as the development planning machinery consisted primarily of the Executive Council and a small cadre of administrative officers, there was an inclination to concentrate on short-term problems cast generally within the over-all framework of colonial policy.

There was little inclination during the interwar period to make significant alterations in the existing state of affairs. Once the economy and administration had been reestablished there seemed little cause to establish and execute plans designed to remodel the territory drastically. However, it was not only the absence of a crisis situation that disinclined the colonial governments to "plan." Possibly of equal significance were the nearly insurmountable problems that large-scale planning necessarily entailed. The expatriate administrative staff in Tanganyika, for example, during this period was exceedingly small. In 1930 there were fewer than 1,000 expatriate civil servants (excluding railway personnel and military) in this country of 363,000 square miles, or fewer than one for every 363 square miles.[7] Not only was the administration overburdened, but it was completely without experience in the planning field. While there may have existed a handful of farsighted administrators in the capital city and Executive Council, the major concern of the provincial administration, which in British-African territories long dominated policy-making, was the maintenance of law and order and the collection of taxes in proper indirect rule style.

Indirect rule relies upon a massive tier of native administrators (a hierarchy of chiefs, clerks, court attendants, etc.) with a minimum of training and education. National planning, however, ultimately requires large-scale alteration in mass behavior and preferably in the values and meanings that men associate with their behavior. Stated otherwise, the implementation of large-scale economic and social welfare planning requires considerable administrative skill and capacity of a modern variety at the local level. The extension of such an administrative cadre at the provincial, district, and even lower levels had to wait for a radical change in the basis of administration, which did not occur until the immediate postwar period and which required the dismantling of the indirect rule system of administration. Babu Niculescu writes:

The administrative background to planning . . . has thus been the dual one of a geographically decentralized regional or district administration involving a staff of self-sufficing and isolated non-specialists, and of specialized but also isolated departments at the center.[8]

The structure of the political system itself discouraged planning at this early period in still another way. Decisions to plan systematically for significant changes in the people and landscape of Tanganyika necessarily had to be made in London, but once they were made by the Colonial Office it was necessary that the detailed formulation and execution of the plan be carried out in Tanganyika. The communication, and ideological, gap between Great Smith Street and Government House in Dar es Salaam served to discourage effective planning severely.

ROLE OF CONSENSUS

We have already touched upon the general relation of planning and popular consensus. Although consensus was not requisite to the maintenance of political leadership in the colonial era so long as the coercive capacity of the colonial power existed, consensus was required if the new norms implicit in the plans were to be widely conformed to. Thus, the difficulty in the colonial period of determining the popular will and of securing the consent of those who would be required, by altering their values and behavior, to give final implementation to the plan also effectively served to discourage planning on a large scale. Popular consultation had to await the prior development of a political organization and political party system capable of reflecting the essence of popular will and of educating the masses to the necessity for change.

Further, the very nature of the colonial territorial division of the country did little to encourage systematic economic planning. The cadre of administrators and lines of administrative authority, even if they had been sufficient in numbers and sophistication to implement a plan, rarely administered areas coinciding with regions that would have lent themselves to efficient planning and development.

An interesting and insightful contrast of the insular economics of the West Indies to the few isolated and economically productive clusters of people in the vast African territories was recently suggested by Babu Niculescu.[9] He noted that the problems of planning the economic development of both isolated Caribbean islands and parochial isolated pockets of productivity in the sparsely settled African territories are surprisingly alike. In Kenya, as well as in Tanganyika, early *ad hoc* planning as reflected in the annual budget shows an attempt to develop a communications superstructure sufficient to link the insular pockets of productive commercial agriculture to the capital city and export market. In this respect planning in the early stages was in the interest of that element of the population involved in commercial agriculture, which at this stage in Kenya and Tanganyika included very few Africans. In Uganda, however, African peasant cash-cropping developed much earlier. This early development is reflected in the significantly larger investment in an extensive rural road network that even today is far superior to that of either Kenya or Tanganyika. The tendency of the little deliberate planning that did occur to focus upon facilitating export commodities was consistent with the fiscal, and particularly with the revenue, philosophy of government in much of British Africa during this period. The procedure for drafting the budget required the financial secretary to project forecasts of revenue from taxation. As noted above, the primary source of revenue was customs and import duties, and a major dependence upon this source of revenue led to an almost unconscious and continuing effort to encourage enterprise that would increase exports and thereby help cover the costs of administration.

BUDGETARY AND ECONOMIC POLICY

A statement of fiscal philosophy by a colonial secretary of the interwar period is indicative of the thinking that characterized Colonial Office policy at the time: "A colony should have only those services which it can afford to maintain out of its own resource." Granted that an influential element in the Colonial Office no longer regarded colonies as a paying proposition, there were nevertheless during this era very few who were so bold as to feel that the metropolis should provide the dependency with a wide range of subsidized services. This attitude was reflected in the budgetary process; it was a cardinal principle of colonial administration that there should not be a deficit. The colonial governments in the interwar period were able to raise loans with relatively little difficulty, in part because their efforts to do so were often backstopped by the British government. It was assumed that the proper source of funds, however, was the London Stock Market and procedures to expedite such loans were provided for in the Colonial Stock Acts of 1877 and 1900.

Much to the distress of fiscal purists in the Colonial Office, conditions in Tanganyika were so critical after the departure of the Germans and the assumption of authority by Great Britain that it was necessary for the United Kingdom Treasury to grant funds (albeit very small) directly to the territorial government. This chaotic state of Tanganyika's finances precluded floating loans on the London market under the provisions of the Colonial Stock Act. Instead it was necessary to secure government guarantees for loans, and this in turn necessitated special Parliamentary approval—certainly not an economical way to secure financial resources. It is worth noting, however, that until 1925, when Tanganyika was able to finance her own budget for the first time, the greater part of the deficits were met by loans and the smaller part by direct grants.

Two additional factors contribute significantly to the philosophy of fiscal noninvolvement and the absence of planning during this period. In the first instance the novel theories of Keynesian economics were either rejected outright or had not yet been directed toward questions of colonial development. More important, however, were the times themselves. The immediate post-First World War era for all East Africa, but for Tanganyika in particular, was one not of development but of restoration. Only about three years separate the date when a Tanganyika budget first became self-supporting and the onset of the depression. In neither period was it possible for the United Kingdom to consider the extraordinary expenditure that development planning on any substantial scale would have required.

The type and source of external aid to Tanganyika during this early period is shown in some detail below. The dependence upon loans and the burden of debt service are revealing. The profits of imperialism were often intangible and frequently depended upon a monopoly of the money market. When a territorial budget of less than two million pounds expends nearly half a million for debt service, it is not likely that sizable local sources capable of financing internal development will be available. Thus, a forced dependence upon loans, in the absence of grants-in-aid, not only reflected a United Kingdom antidevelopment planning attitude but acted to limit severely a capacity for purely territorially financed development, as minor as it would likely have been.

TABLE 2A

TYPES AND SOURCES OF EXTERNAL AID

Date	Type of Loan or Grant	Interest	Amount In Pounds
1920–22	Grant-in-aid		403,000
1922–25	Loan	5%	3,135,000
1928	Guaranteed Loan	4.5%	2,070,000
1931	Guaranteed Loan	4%	3,000,000
1932	Guaranteed Loan	4%	500,000
1930–38	Grant		214,000
		Total	9,322,000

Source: Colonial Office Records

TABLE 2B

ALLOCATIONS TO THE RAILWAY FROM
THE LOAN FUNDS SHOWN IN TABLE 2A

Date	Type of Loan or Grant	Interest	Amount In Pounds
1922–25	Loan	5%	1,700,000
1928	Guaranteed Loan	4.5%	1,800,000
1931	Guaranteed Loan	4%	2,200,000
		Total for Railways	5,700,000

Source: Colonial Office Records

The fact that Tanganyika, like other colonial territories, was not in control of its own monetary policy acted to limit severely its capacity to employ expansionary fiscal measures to cope with problems of restoration or depression, not to speak of development. Between 1925 and 1931 recurrent revenue increased by only 8 per cent, while by 1932 recurrent expenditure annually was running in the neighborhood of 300,000 pounds. Indicative of the attitude toward development is the fact that both recurrent deficit and capital expenditure were balanced almost entirely by external loans, with the subsequent imposition of carrying charges.

A look at the sources and nature of locally derived revenue during this period is useful, for it demonstrates both the inflexibility and the poverty of the local resources vis-à-vis a capacity for development planning. Up to 1945 the principal direct taxes levied by the Tanganyika government were the native poll tax, non-native poll tax, municipal tax, and licenses. Indirect taxes consisted primarily of import duties, export duties, excise and sugar consumption tax.

The effective levy and collection of a poll tax has long been *sine qua non* of effective administration. The relation of this tax to the extension of metropolitan hegemony into the interior of the East African territories and its relation to the necessity of demonstrating the omnipresence of imperial authority and achieving administrative self-sufficiency is a story that has never been completely or adequately told. For, like most fiscal devices, its inspiration and purpose were, in the first instance, certainly as much political as they were economic. The imposition of the tax was often undertaken in order to force a money economy upon a primitive people by requiring them to grow and sell cash crops, if for no other reason than to pay taxes so as to contribute to the costs of their own administration. This political aspect of the poll tax was particularly important in the early days of Tanganyika when there was a substitution not only of British for German administrators, but also of legalized taxation for arbitrary tribute. In the first stages of occupation, however, and in the absence of a money economy, the poll tax was collected in kind, e.g., skins, ivory, foodstuffs. The early district reports describing in excruciating and often pungent detail the stockpiling of decaying animal and vegetable taxes is as humorous to the reader today as it must have been infuriating to the district officer of an earlier period.

Until the opening of the Second World War the poll tax collected by the hierarchy of chiefs, with each level receiving its "feel," was uniquely dependent upon the maintenance of this peculiarly Tanganyikan version of the principle of indirect rule. During this early period the poll tax accounted for more than a third of total revenue. Failure to alter this obviously retrogressive tax is but additional evidence that policy during this era was one of inaction:

planning not to plan. The Tanganyikan revenue system was similar to those of Kenya and Uganda, although Tanganyika had the distinction of providing the earliest evidence of a disposition toward fiscal experimentation. Attached to the poll tax was a special levy on plural wives which the missionary interest groups thought would discourage multiple marriages. However, as they might have anticipated, a tax of two shillings per wife did little either to swell the territorial treasury or to dissuade those able to afford more than one wife to forego the pleasures and advantages that polygamy had demonstrated for so long. The noble experiment was abandoned in 1939. The municipal tax was in reality a property tax based upon the annual rental value of the holdings and assessed in a manner comparable to that in the United Kingdom. In common with other East African territories, it applied only to gazetted cities and townships.

TRANSNATIONAL BASIS OF DEVELOPMENT

The Versailles Treaty and the deliberations of the Mandates Commission as to the exact terms of the agreement as it affected Tanganyika required an open-door trade policy comparable to that included in the famed Congo Basin Treaty. This policy was not without its liabilities for a primary producing territory such as Tanganyika. Without reciprocal trade agreements, in an era notorious for such associations, it was the importer of Tanganyikan produce and not Tanganyika that benefited by a free-trade policy. Although free competition among imports reduced some prices, this advantage was more often offset by the problem of obtaining satisfactory outlets for Tanganyikan exports. It is not surprising that the free-trade policy for Tanganyika, like the Congo Basin Agreement, disintegrated during the depression and that Tanganyika's tariff policy subsequently fell into line with those of the other East African states. It is also worth noting that tariffs were limited under the mandate to 10 per cent *ad valorem*. This low and inflexible rate provided an inadequate source of revenue during periods of expansion and insufficient centralized control of imports during recessions.

It is already evident that Tanganyika, viewed either as a land mass or as a people, until 1961 had never experienced a national or independent status. Its economy and administration, as well as its planning and nonplanning, have always been dictated externally.

Even more significant is the continued international dependency of Tanganyika after independence. National planning for all states in the interdependent world in which we now live is necessarily transnational, but it has not always been so; however, dependency has been the rule for Tanganyika from the moment of its existence as a distinct territory and people.

The transnational nature of the planning process can be demonstrated as early as 1923 when Tanganyika, for political as much as for economic reasons, joined with Kenya and Uganda in a modified customs union. In fact, one can trace the volatile and frequently violent movement toward closer union in East Africa to this customs union of 1923, for it signified that Tanganyika's political and economic future was to be henceforth more closely aligned to that of British East Africa than to the League of Nations or to the world community generally. In 1927 this union was strengthened by the addition of a further agreement which eliminated tariffs between the three territories. This, however, raised a serious problem of economic association that has persisted to the present and one that still acts to discourage closer economic and political union. Tanganyika was, and still is, economically the least developed of the three territories. Thus, exports by Kenya to Tanganyika in particular are relatively large, and to the extent that Tanganyika relies for its imports on Kenya and Uganda it sacrifices substantial customs revenue.

Symptomatic of this problem of uneven economic yoking is the sugar consumption tax and the anomaly over butter. For instance, when Kenya was unable to meet Tanganyika's requirements for butter during the 1930's, it was necessary to import butter from elsewhere. However, the joint tariff on butter imports, in order to protect Kenya's agriculture, was so high that demands for butter declined precipitously.[10] It was not until the establishment of the East African High Commission and the formation of an effective customs union that such problems were at least partially solved.

ROLE OF FOREIGN TRADE AND REVENUE

Export taxes along with import duties have always loomed large in the fiscal picture and must be examined historically if we are to develop an adequate understanding of the over-all situation. As is well recognized, this tax is attractive, for it is generally easy to levy. However, it is equally well known that it is subject to the vagaries of world trade and is an inherently unpredictable and unstable source of revenue. Sharp fluctuations in available government resources and subsequent expenditures in the new nations that have inherited the luxury of a political opposition are dangerous indeed, for they provide an excellent opportunity for an opposition party or faction to demand that it be given the opportunity to govern. Some new nations have found it easier to neutralize and silence a political opposition than to forego dependence on this politically dangerous revenue base. Not only is the tax indirect, but it is indiscriminate, for in a peasant economy it is the small farmer who inevitably shoulders the major burden. Further, there exists the perennial problem of fixing rates that will not discourage production but will yield a worthwhile and predictable return.

The significance of major dependence upon export taxes is twofold. The dependence of government upon this source of income has encouraged, if not required, government involvement and control of the marketing of export commodities. This in turn has frequently required administrative control at the earlier stages of planting and harvesting. It is only a short step from regulating the planting, harvesting, and marketing of crops to the formation of a comprehensive and powerful marketing board. In short, major dependence on an export tax for revenue has been a powerful force working toward implicit and often uncoordinated government planning of the major sector of the economy. Of related significance has been the increasing recognition by governments of the necessity of controlling prices paid to the producers so as to build in a stabilizing factor sufficient to maintain political stability. Each trend, of course, has been reinforced by the other. Thus, while external policy was one of nonplanning, there were at work within the economy and the political system of Tanganyika forces inevitably moving toward a highly planned polity and economy. Often the unanticipated consequences of human actions are of the most significance.

This survey of fiscal policy during the interwar period has demonstrated a variety of relevant trends and forces that have their origins in this era. The over-all revenue policy further illustrates the problems facing a government seeking to maintain a balanced budget in an only partially monetized economy which of necessity relies heavily on external finance and import duties for internal development. A more detailed view of these early trends contributing to a planned polity and economy despite authoritative decisions not to plan can be gained through a survey of foreign trade during these crucial decades.

TABLE 3

FISCAL ASPECTS OF EXPORTS AND IMPORTS IN TANGANYIKA, 1929–35
(Thousands of Pounds)

	1929	1930	1931	1932	1933	1934	1935
Nongovernment							
Trade Imports	3,743	1,868	2,000	1,749	1,868	2,241	2,854
Government Imports	542	78	495	122	79	101	135
Total	4,285	1,946	2,495	1,871	1,947	2,342	2,989
Domestic Imports							
(from Kenya and Uganda)	3,722	2,543	1,645	2,190	2,543	2,645	3,445
Re-exports							
(to Kenya and Uganda)	265	182	245	166	182	211	278
Total	3,987	2,725	1,890	2,356	2,725	2,856	3,723
Customs Duties	739	565	411	*	404	476	612
Revenue Budget	1,992	1,749	1,522	*	1,564	1,720	1,973

* Change in financial year makes figures not comparable.

Source: Colonial Office Records

Colonial Office policy toward trade was generally consistent with its over-all laissez-faire attitude, and little evidence exists that fiscal measures were ever deliberately employed to develop or control trade. Trade, it was felt, would seek its own equilibrium.

The slow rate of development, which was as much a product of policy inertia as it was of deliberate nonplanning, generally led to an imbalance between imports and exports. This divergent trend resulted in a mounting export surplus. As government was the major importer, it alone had the capacity to bring these two factors into line. However, government expenditure on imports was dictated not by a development plan, or even by the scale of exports, but purely by the requirements of budgetary policy. There is little doubt that the absence of regulatory machinery for the control of trade considerably damaged and slowed the process and capacity for development.

Whereas the Tanganyikan government had some control over the ratio of imports to exports, which it chose not to exercise, it had no control over the issuance of currency, which also might have been employed to give impetus to development. Considering the sizable interest paid on Tanganyika's loans in the London market, it is not surprising that Tanganyika's currency was issued jointly with the rest of East Africa by the London-based East Africa Currency Board. This board did not possess the prerogative, however, of creating money, nor could it regulate or expend credit; for interest rates, as they affected credit and currency expansion, were regulated by the Banking Ordinance's control over reserve requirements. In effect, then, varying rates and encouraging credit expansion were not visible monetary instruments available to the territorial government during this period.

INDIRECT RULE AND DIVIDE-AND-RULE

For a variety of reasons Great Britain, as noted above, has emphasized administration and development at the local level in contrast to other metropolitan powers. This policy is so complex as to preclude its full treatment here. However, certain particularly relevant aspects must be noted. Indirect rule, a philosophy born of the necessity of ruling vast areas with a minimum of metropolitan manpower and resources, accounts in part for the early concentration of resources on provincial administration. It was also evident that the creation, or perpetuation, of tribal, regional, or other spatial and ethnic differences, provided a form of internal tension that could be manipulated to insure continued control and contribute to a capacity to cope with isolated incidents of rebellion. Divide-and-rule, therefore, was a natural outgrowth of the philosophy of indirect rule. When it was apparent that plans to disengage from Tanganyika would be required, the British, drawing from their own culture and heritage, gave extraordinary emphasis to the necessity of developing a solid substructure of local government. Further, the concentration of administrative resources at the local level built up, through time, a vested interest in development from below, and it is not surprising that a prestigeful and relatively large provincial administration lobbied effectively for constantly larger investments in local government and development.

During the period under discussion the "native authorities" (units of indirect rule), consisting generally of a chief, or a chief in council, received a rebate on the poll tax collected and had some limited authority to raise additional revenue from licenses and services. Additional revenue was also obtained from minor refunds and from the surplus balances of certain central government marketing operations. However, this latter source of revenue did not loom large until after the war and the emergence of modern local government.

Minor development locally was undertaken during this period primarily through the provision of a revolving local fund, employed for local authority's capital works. The fund consisted of the total surplus balances of the native local authorities. As it rarely exceeded 100,000 pounds it was unable to provide development funds on a scale that prevailed in Kenya and Uganda, where loan funds for local governments were a regular part of the budget allocation of the central government.

III

The Wartime Crisis and the Genesis of Planning

We must return from the locality in Tanganyika to the United Kingdom to discern the first steps toward systematic planning as they affected Tanganyika. After the First World War, the British Treasury spent a considerable sum to help the various dependencies recuperate and re-establish order.[1] However, the variable fortunes of political parties and party philosophies in the United Kingdom significantly affected views on the nature and seriousness of the obligations linking colony and metropolis. In 1929, for example, the newly installed Labor government anticipated a later era by passing a colonial development act empowering government to spend up to 1,000,000 pounds a year on colonial development over an eleven-year period, of which nearly 9,000,000 pounds were in fact expended.[2] Between 1931 and 1938 Tanganyika received 214,000 pounds from this source. The significance of this plan and fund, however, lies not in its magnitude but in the stimulus it gave to research, to the improvement of statistics, and thus to an improved capacity to forecast revenue and expenditure.

SOME EARLY BEGINNINGS

The modern era of planning began in 1940 with the passage of the Colonial Development and Welfare Act. The passage of this act and the debate that surrounded it clearly indicate the capacity of a crisis situation to trigger man's rational energies to restore order by seeking to establish an improved state of affairs by first postulating and defining the goal and then laying down the stages re-

26

quired for its realization. The Colonial Development and Welfare Act was born of an economic crisis culminating in serious rioting in the British West Indies. The Moyne Commission, after investigating these disturbances in 1938, recommended that its proposals, which subsequently gave rise to the Colonial Development and Welfare Act, should apply not only to the West Indies but to the colonial territories generally. This in itself was evidence of a developing inclination to think systematically and to anticipate general colonial problems. Obviously the Colonial Development and Welfare Act during the war years was little more than a declaration of intent. It is fair to say that it was largely politically inspired to encourage the dependent territories to cast their lot with the Empire and forego thoughts of taking advantage of the war to embarrass Great Britain. From 1940 to 1945 less than 3 million pounds were spent even though 5 million had been authorized.[3] The spirit of this act could only be made effective after the war, and in 1945 the colonial secretary proposed to give effect to the program by establishing an Advisory Economic Policy Committee, special advisory bodies to the separate colonial governments, and an over-all clearinghouse for statistics and data to be located in London. It was under the terms of this act that Tanganyika received support for its first (1944) Development Plan which envisaged an expenditure of 12.5 million pounds over three years, with the principal allocations designated for natural resources, social services, and communications. The significance of this initial plan, however, lies in the promise it gave of things to come; for reasons noted below, it was never implemented and was superseded by the plan of 1946.

The war impressed on Asian and African nationalists, as well as leaders of the metropolitan powers, the fact that a new era was dawning and that the postwar period would inevitably witness the development of new forms of relations between the metropolis and the dependent territories. Anticipating this era and the successful conclusion of the war, in 1945 the British government signaled the commencement of what we have here termed "planned disengagement" by requesting ten-year development plans from the various colonial territories. The financial crisis of 1947 in Britain curtailed these bold plans for systematic investment and expenditure in the colonies. As Niculescu has perceptively noted, however, it had another implication that significantly molded British colonial policy, as contrasted, for example, with that of France. It became "an accepted tenet in London" and also "for the local officials dealing with planning and development problems in the various territories concerned, that welfare and social development have to be paid for out of the resources of each territory and that therefore an increase in productive resources must be the main purpose of development." [4]

POLITICS OF CLOSER UNION

Before moving to the current period covered in this background of national planning in Tanganyika, it is important to set the stage further by drawing attention to some of the political and wartime factors that significantly affected later events.

When Tanganyika came under effective British rule in 1921, the white settlers' vision of an Empire was given renewed impetus. Maneuvering for and against the union of Tanganyika, Uganda, and Kenya has characterized the politics of this region ever since. The white settlers, especially the numerous Kenya planters, sought closer union. They were given considerable support by commercial and Empire interests in the United Kingdom. However, the movement was opposed by Africans generally, and more particularly by those in Uganda, who feared extension of white domination into their territory. Liberal elements in the United Kingdom opposed it, too.[5]

Two major commissions of inquiry signaled the movement toward union. The Ormsby-Gore Commission of 1925 and the Hilton-Young Commission of 1930 were concerned with two major issues. First, they investigated and then sought to accommodate interests for and against closer political and economic union between Tanganyika, Kenya, and Uganda. Second, they dealt with the position of the immigrant community and particularly with that of the dominant Europeans. Both commissions, to the chagrin of some members, were bound by the statement of the secretary of state for the colonies in 1923 that Britain was committed in Kenya to the paramountcy of African interests. Thus, the Hilton-Young Commission found that a conflict existed between what it considered a desirable form of closer union and the settlers' interpretation of their position within such a union.

The existence of white settlers in East Africa has, of course, always complicated, if not dominated, the political scene, but it has also introduced a factor into the economy that might not otherwise have existed. Land was developed by the settlers on a large scale and thereby came to have a value which in turn contributed to the mobilization of additional capital resources. In Tanganyika few freehold land titles were granted by the administering power, and land policy generally was much more restrictive than in Kenya. All aspects of political and economic development, in Tanganyika as well as in Uganda and Kenya, either implicitly or explicitly have depended in considerable degree on the existing and proposed level of association and union among the three territories.

The historical antecedents and similarity of organizational tactics and motivation that surround this thorny issue of closer union in East Africa have remained constant even though the players have changed. It is worth noting that the history of attempts to amalgamate the lands of East Africa does not begin, as is often thought, with the First World War or with the British mandate over Tanganyika in 1921. The Sultan of Oman, and later of Zanzibar, schemed and planned to extend Arab control into the interior and to unify the hinterlands with the coast. The German East Africa Society once had visions of a greater East Africa extending outward from Tanganyika. The Portuguese, too, looked forward to the eventual linkage of a number of coastal settlements; and, as is well known, Cecil Rhodes dreamed aloud of a "Rule Britannia from the Cape to Cairo." A history viewed from the interior of East Africa would note the extensive treaty relationships and holdings of the Hehe and Haya kingdoms in Tanganyika or of the empire of Kitara, whose domain once extended into regions now part of Tanganyika, Uganda, and Kenya. A historical view shows quite clearly that the problems and plans for an East African union are continuous through time. There have been, over the past half-century, a number of commissions, conferences, white papers, and that peculiarly British device, "the inquiry," investigating the nature and desirability of union in East Africa.

The men who now gather to discuss this problem speak with a different accent and are of a different color from those of a decade ago, for power to deliberate this issue has shifted from one group to the other. But the process is familiar; the kinds of arguments favoring and opposing federation are like those of yesterday, and the obstacles to union are the ones that have been there for some time. For example, Uganda historically, fearing to compromise her protectorate status, has held back from federation. More recently federation has been opposed for fear that it would jeopardize Buganda's special federal status in an independent Uganda. A continual problem, not yet solved, in planning for union in East Africa has been the differential political status of the prospective constituents. Uganda is a federated dominion containing constituent monarchies, whereas Tanganyika is a unitary republic. Political alterations, by the very nature of the essence of things political, differentially affect the fortunes and well-being of men. Changing the relation of space to authority may be sought in one instance to enhance and perpetuate the rule of those possessed of predominant influence, or it may reflect a change in the locus of predominant influence. In either case the change would be resisted by that segment or interest of the people whose relative position it would adversely affect. The basis of community within the context of the "state" in East Africa has been largely that of race, and proposals for federation and closer union have been inspired largely by racial interest and would have differentially affected the fortunes of the respective racial communities. It is important to note, however, that the constituent elements affected by alterations in the relation of space to authority are not necessarily race, and when the basis of constituent community comes to be something other than race, the locus of support, as well as of opposition to union, will probably change accordingly. There are already numerous indications that this is in fact the case.

With the conclusion of the war and recognition that the political evolution of the colonies was inevitable, Great Britain sought to put her colonial house in order so as to render the process of disengagement as painless and profitable as possible. In 1945 an administrative union of Tanganyika, Uganda, and Kenya was proposed by the British government to consist of a high commission of the respective territorial governors and a central legislative assembly. In the last days of 1947 the British government issued an order in council establishing the East African High Commission as a supraterritorial authority possessed of its own constitution, powers, and distinct functions. The Central Legislative Assembly was empowered to legislate on matters concerning those services falling under the responsibility of the High Commission: e.g., income tax administration, defense, harbors and railways, the University of East Africa, research, posts and telegraphs, and communications. The High Commission was responsible for aviation, railroads and harbors, posts and telegraphs, defense, research and statistical services, Lake Victoria fisheries, meteorological services, and customs and excise tax (collection and allocation only). Although it had no police or tax powers, the High Commission had many of the attributes of a federal system. Independence of Tanganyika in December 1961, Uganda in 1962, and Kenya in 1963 has resulted in the replacement of the East African High Commission by the East African Common Services Organization. Kenya, Uganda, and Tanganyika participate equally in this new association and responsibility is in the hands of the three respective national leaders. The functions of the organization have been divided into four groups: communication, commercial and industrial coordination, finance, and social and research services. Policy formulation for each of the four functional segments is the responsibility of three ministers, one from each territory. The new Central Legislative Assembly is composed of the twelve ministers noted above, plus nine representative members from each country, elected by their respective legislatures, as well as a secretary-general and a legal secretary.

The future of the Common Services Organization is much in doubt. Whether it will evolve into a true federation of East Africa, as urged by most East African leaders publicly, or whether it will disintegrate in the face of a hardening of national boundaries it is not yet possible to foresee.

Although the above summary of the nature of the legal association of Tanganyika with the rest of East Africa is insufficient for most purposes, it does provide an overview of the long-standing substance and historical ties that of necessity must be taken into account in the formulation of plans for Tanzania. Further, the frontiers of Tanganyika, established as they were in Berlin in 1890, pay little regard to the location of natural economic or cultural regions, and as a consequence the natural intercourse and trade of large parts of the country are with neighboring states. The Lake Victoria region, for example, is to a certain extent a natural economic and communications region, and the relatively heavily popu-

lated Lake and Northern Provinces look to Lake Victoria and the
Uganda-Kenya Railways to Nairobi and Mombasa for their external lines of communication. Thus, a customs union with Kenya
and Uganda was probably inevitable. It is not, however, without
its disadvantages for Tanzania. Kenya is the most economically and
industrially developed of the three territories, and not only is
Nairobi the headquarters of the Common Services Organization
and Central Legislature, but it tends to be the focal point for other
interterritorial associations of a public and private nature. More
important, the relatively highly developed nature of Kenya serves
to attract additional private capital investment to the relative dis-
advantage of Tanzania and Uganda. So long as industry in Kenya
and Uganda has a long lead on Tanzania, it is unlikely, short of
national customs barriers, that Tanzania will develop an industrial
complex at a very rapid rate. "From Tanganyika's point of view the
problem is how the advantages of the common market can be
preserved without unduly prejudicing such industrial development
as would be feasible and desirable if Tanganyika were to be considered in isolation." [6]

THE SECOND WORLD WAR AND PLANNING POLICY

The opening of the Second World War and the explicit inten-
tions of Nazi Germany to re-establish its position in East Africa
gave added impetus to union but also placed a moratorium on
organizational and constitutional movements to achieve that end.
With respect to other wartime activities relative to this survey, it
is difficult to obtain specific data for so little was published or made
available. No doubt a careful study of secretariat files would bring
much information to light. Nevertheless, it is possible to discuss
at least three features of wartime policy which had an impact on
postwar planning.

A need for produce-marketing control can hardly be disputed
during a war. However, this requirement not only extended to
control over British consumption but also was designed as a means
of obtaining scarce dollars. Controls as they affected Tanganyika
had a number of effects. For example, new products were introduced into the territory as sources of traditional supplies were
overrun by the enemy. Large surpluses were accumulated because

of the curbs on imports. Most important, however, was the introduction of extensive controls over marketing and production. The postwar Labor government was impressed by the benefits that could be derived from highly controlled colonial marketing. Sir Stafford Cripps stated in 1948 that "it will clearly be a great help to colonial producers in any plans to increase the volume of their production if they have assurance of a market for their goods for some years to come."[7] Further, the end of wartime controls made it increasingly difficult to continue bulk purchases with accompanying guaranteed prices to producers.

The Ministry of Food in the United Kingdom experienced increasing difficulty in setting an equitable basis for purchase agreements. As trading conditions changed, the ministry found it increasingly more advantageous to allow wartime contracts to expire and to purchase on the world market. This permitted the Territorial Marketing Boards to operate on their own account as the sole sellers of their country's products. The debate over the equity and economic benefits of this system have been endless, with the main criticism being leveled at the massive surpluses of the West African Marketing Board. In general, economists have opposed the system, while governments have defended the scheme on the basis of administrative expediency.

In Tanganyika only one of the three principal export crops, cotton, was marketed in this way. In the immediate postwar era cotton was sold under contract to the Raw Cotton Commission in Britain. In 1952 Tanganyika established its own Lint and Seed Marketing Board, which fixed prices a year in advance to ginners and growers with surplus funds being paid into the Price Assistance Fund. Sisal, the major export crop, was subject to bulk purchase by the Board of Trade until 1948, after which the estate owners established their own marketing cooperative.

Coffee, although controlled in Uganda and Kenya, never came under monopoly marketing in the same way in Tanganyika, in large part because of the existence of an efficient plantation organization, The Tanganyika Coffee Growers Association, which encouraged African cooperatives to use its services.

Tanganyika has contributed a unique chapter to the history of large-scale planning. The colossal failure of the immediate postwar groundnut scheme is treated in some detail here, because of its

unique flavor and because its legacy has substantially affected national planning in Tanganyika ever since.

PEANUTS, THE THINGS OF WHICH DREAMS ARE FASHIONED

Africa has always tempted men to try the impossible. Its very
massiveness and hidden mysteries have challenged missionaries,
empire-builders, and explorers alike. Close upon the war's end it
occurred to representatives of the United Africa Company, a
Unilever subsidiary, that the acute shortage of fats and edible oils
in Britain might be solved by planting thousands of acres of relatively unoccupied eastern and central Africa with groundnuts. The
idea caught hold in the Colonial Office and Ministry of Foods, and
men who for nearly ten years had had to limit their ambitions and
imaginations to the exigencies of a war were finally free to "think
big" for peaceful purposes. Once again the colonies would help
in the restoration of the mother country. The plan, as it evolved
in its early stages under the general supervision of the Ministry of
Foods, seemed to view the land and people of Tanganyika as an
inert and fertile garden susceptible to and eagerly awaiting the plans
and schemes of Englishmen. With un-British boldness and audacity,
which we might charge to war fatigue and boredom, they called for
clearing not thousands but three million acres of tsetse-infested,
relatively uninhabited land and the subsequent planting of this
virgin soil with groundnuts. Three million acres is nearly five thousand square miles, a land area considerably larger than all of
Connecticut or Puerto Rico or Lebanon. The initial scheme called
for dividing the three million acres into thirty-thousand-acre units
located in selected eastern and central African areas but primarily
in Tanganyika. Elspeth Huxley described the plan:

> Will they do it? If not in this generation, they say, then in the
> next. They intend to breed their own type of homoindus-
> trialensis. For their clerks and tractor-drivers will have chil-
> dren, and these children will be de-wormed, fed on Paludrine,
> and sent to school, and in their schools the transmutation will
> be effected. When they have come to man's estate, healthy,
> instructed and versed in co-operation, they will come into the
> groundnut inheritance, with its three million acres of cultiva-

tion, its fleets of tractors and implements, its laboratories and hospitals, its workshops and schools, its network of transport, and its ties with world-wide markets. In such a society tribalism, peasantry, superstition, indirect rule, all will have atrophied and died, and the New African will inherit a new earth.[8]

The Overseas Food Corporation, with initial capital of 15,000,-000 pounds, was the public body created to give effect to this daring venture. It was originally estimated that the over-all capital expenditure for the scheme would run about 25,000,000 pounds. By 1954 the scheme required that 600,000 acres be under cultivation. It is worth noting that a United Nations mission visiting Tanganyika in that year reported slightly less than 150,000 acres in the Central Province and 180,000 in the Northern Province not under cultivation but designated for clearance and cultivation.

The plan seemed excellent in many ways, for the investment required to implement the program would in turn contribute enormously to Tanganyika's economy, long recognized as one of the least developed in the world. A scheme of these dimensions, it was thought, could not help but give rise to additional development, new communications facilities, and an enormous expansion in road and rail construction. The infrastructure of the plan called for building a new ocean port and railway in the Southern Province. The planners foresaw not only a long-starved England supplied with an abundance of protein and margarine, but also the building up of whole new towns, schools, technical training centers, and hospitals in Tanganyika. Thus, Tanganyika, by helping the United Kingdom, would be helping itself.

By mid-1947 a small army of men with machines and high hopes began to advance into the interior of Tanganyika. In less than a year of preliminary operations, the scheme had managed to spend nearly eight million pounds at a rate approaching a million pounds a month. Excitement and enthusiasm in about equal proportion to confusion characterized the implementation of this grand design.

A consignment of Sherman tanks, which Messrs. Vickers-Armstrong have been asked to convert into agricultural tractors without preliminary experimentation under African conditions, was landed in the Southern Province without proper facilities for delivery at the scene of operations.[9]

The whole exercise had about it an air of a military campaign, with the Panzer forces of the Overseas Food Corporation led by former British Army generals leading the blitzkrieg against a stubborn Tanganyika along a wide front. Like the Russian winter, however, the Southern Province of Tanganyika wreaked havoc on the machines and plans of these alien men. The major area of operations was in the Kongwa region of the Central Province. During the first year in this region, the plan called for clearing and planting 150,000 acres. By the end of that year less than 14,000 acres had been cleared and about half of that sown with groundnuts.[10] In characteristic British understatement one observer concluded that "in view of the huge scale of operations, the fact that there had been no preliminary agricultural experimentation was disastrous." [11]

Neither the former military personnel nor the impatient Ministry of Food planners were able even to come close to clearing the huge tracts of land according to schedule. Everything seemed to go wrong. The huge land-clearing machines brought into Tanganyika at tremendous expense and labor failed to do the job. The transport infrastructure was a serious bottleneck. The heavy equipment choked the limited docking facilities of Dar es Salaam. Even when the equipment and supplies arrived in Dar es Salaam on time and cleared the harbor, they often overburdened the single narrow-gauge rail line and then on occasion bogged down in the mud and dust of the near-roadless hinterland. To make matters worse, it was discovered, after clearing vast tracts, that the soil in some areas would not support intensive groundnut agriculture.

To our knowledge no record exists of the attitude of the African as he watched this massive assault upon his land, which the gods had long before assured him was a fickle and vengeful mistress at best. Although the Wagogo peasant and cattle people of this region were not in possession of rainfall statistics, as were the European planners, they knew that average rainfall statistics could only be misleading and that annual and seasonal variations could drown a new crop one year and turn the countryside to dust the following, as they had for centuries past. Had the eager planners learned the language of the Wagogo and listened closely to their minstrels tell of years of famine, they might have been less optimistic than they were. The seasonal quality of the rain, plus the composition of the soil, turned the ground during much of the year into a concrete-like substance that not only ruthlessly dulled plowshares but taxed heavy clearing, planting, and harvesting machinery beyond expectation and endurance. Unpredictable rainfall, inefficiency of machines designed for a different climate and soil, and a combination of other human and environmental failures reduced the yield per acre from a planned seven hundred pounds of groundnuts to about two hundred.[12]

Elspeth Huxley, who visited the scheme at the height of its activity, wrote that "no one really knows what will emerge from that ocean of thorns: health or sickness, fertility or desert, good soil or bad, and, most improtant of all, water or no water. For it is lack of water that has made all this land a wilderness."[13] J. P. Moffett, commenting upon the failure, summed up a little-known tragicomedy as follows:

> Though good relationships between existing inhabitants and the newcomers were maintained, the lack of staff interchange produced a situation not unlike that which would have arisen had the army conducted land maneuvers on the otherwise empty decks of a battleship at sea, the latter representing the established order of things in Tanganyika.[14]

The huge, rusting machines, from a distance resembling grazing elephants, and the obviously man-made scars on the landscape which still show through a new growth of bush bear mute testimony to this noble effort. However, all was not lost. A new port, Mtwara, was constructed and a new rail from there into the interior was built. The smashed hopes, partially cleared land, machinery, and rights to land were eventually turned over to the Tanganyika Agricultural Corporation (TAC). The experiment now consists of the establishment of tenant farming in the hope of effecting, as the governor of Tanganyika put it, "an agricultural revolution for African peasants."[15]

It is calculated that the ill-fated plan at its conclusion in 1952 left fixed assets and expendables valued at about 6 million pounds and had spent 19 million pounds to clear and develop the land.[16]

Another 3.5 million pounds had been granted to the East African Railways and Harbors Administration to finance the building of Mtwara and the new Southern Province rail line. Lord Hailey has remarked: "The more permanent effect has been to provide the territory with an improved stock of capital which though it might have been better utilized from the point of view of the economy . . . was a windfall addition to its resources." [17]

TAC, which inherited the leavings of this colossal failure, has continued to experiment with plantation-type agriculture, but on a much smaller scale and with a view toward developing a new type of African peasant agriculture. The Farming Settlement Scheme, in the words of TAC, "is designed to enable the African peasant cultivator to emerge from the trough of subsistence farming and become a self-reliant and prosperous yeoman farmer able to contribute to the economic development of his native land." [18] TAC inherited three undertakings from the ill-fated groundnut scheme, which it has since developed into experimental peasant agricultural and ranching programs: (a) Nachingwea (Southern Province)—corporation farms and a farming settlement scheme; (b) Urambo (Western Province)—tobacco-growing and farm settlement; and (c) Kongwa (Central Province)—a breeding ranch and farming settlement scheme.[19]

The Farming Settlement Scheme involves the tenancy grant of ten to fifty acres to selected African peasant farmers. Agricultural instruction, marketing facilities, farm machine operations, and other technical aspects of the venture are provided to the participants by the TAC. Despite occasional satisfactory crop yields and the provision of various amenities, the scheme has not proven popular to the African peasant for whose development it was planned. In 1959, after six years of operation of the farming scheme of some fifteen hundred acres in Nachingwea, only five of the original twenty-eight tenants still remained. Of the forty-two tenant farmers who agreed to participate in the scheme in 1953/54, only eleven remained after the fifth year.[20] The total number of tenants reached one hundred and twenty-one in 1955/56 but fell off to seventy-nine in 1958/59.[21]

The farming scheme at Kongwa, which has managed to keep a small part of the ninety thousand acres cleared for groundnuts from returning to bush, "appears to be barely economic at best." [22] And it is estimated that an investment of about thirty thousand pounds is required in equipment to cultivate mechanically the sixteen thousand acres involved in the total plan.[23]

An unanticipated and seldom appreciated consequence of the massive groundnut scheme is the powerful reinforcement it gave to the view that modernization and development for Tanganyika depends upon a nationally planned agricultural revolution. This approach to modernization and nation-building is rarely questioned. Even the *World Bank Report* at its outset states that "the main development task of Tanganyika is to improve the methods of peasant agriculture and cattle keeping." [24]

As the nature of the problems and promises for development and planning that accompanied a wartime situation have been discussed, it is now possible to approach directly the last and major portion of this survey.

IV

Planned Disengagement—Politics and Planning

I can say without hesitation that it is our policy to develop the colonies and all their resources so as to enable their peoples speedily and substantially to improve their economic and social condition, and as soon as may be practical, to obtain responsible self-government. To us the colonies are a great trust and their progress to self-government is a goal towards which his majesty's government will assist them with all means in their power.

These were the words of George Hall, Secretary of State for the Colonies, in July 1946.

THE NEW LOOK

Thought by some, particularly the new Labor government, to be impervious to change, the Colonial Office nevertheless wheeled about to accommodate the new era that dawned at the conclusion of the war. It is interesting to note that readiness to support welfare and educational planning in the colonies came about rather quickly in response to the pressures of African nationalism, whereas an earlier argument for such an approach when made by Keynesian economists and others had little if any effect. The relative autonomy of colonial administration as exercised by the governor and his council in the separate colonies in British Africa, in contrast to French Africa, provided a relatively wide range for developmental experimentation. On this score it is important to recall that the

40

colonial governors and administrators responded to these new forces not only in recognition of the indigenous pressures for change but also because they themselves often tended to identify personally with the territory and its future.

We have already referred to the first development plans drafted in 1944 under the terms of the 1940 Colonial Development and Welfare Act. Tanganyika's plan was not well received by the Colonial Office, for it was felt that too much emphasis had been placed upon social services and welfare. The first postwar plan (1946) profited from the earlier experiences, however, and led to the first explicit statement of economic policy for Tanganyika. According to the Statement of Economic Policy in the *Annual Report* (Tanganyika, 1946):

> The policy aims at increasing the wealth of the territory by the maximum development of its natural resources, with the objective of progressively raising the general standard of living most particularly of the indigenous inhabitants.

In this connection specific reference is made to the following points:

> (a) The interests of economically weak indigenous groups are under constant supervision. In particular these interests are protected by the control of prices, the allocation of essential commodities, the subsidization of essential foodstuffs, where necessary, and by measures taken to safeguard the welfare and to protect the interests of those in paid employment.

> (b) It is the aim of the administrative policy to fit the indigenous inhabitants generally to take over, to the maximum extent possible, the functions of non-indigenous inhabitants in the general economy of the Territory. Educational policy, in which the Technical Training of Africans is given increasing prominence, is directed toward this end.

APPROACHING INDEPENDENCE

Had anyone suggested in 1946 that Tanganyika would be self-governing in 1961, he would have been thought mad. Even the most ardent of the new nationalist leaders thought in much longer terms, though it did not take them as long to rearrange their time schedules as it did the Colonial Office. As late as 1954 a leading European liberal thought that possibly a century would be required. Yet the United Nations visiting missions, much to the outrage of the European Settlers Association, urged independence within a single generation.[1]

The task of creating a state and then developing a nation seemed immense and frightening. In part this reflected the barren harvest of the prewar philosophy of nonplanning. The first U.N. mission to Tanganyika in 1948 remarked that development had been kept to a "bare minimum" and that the territorial budget was merely on a "care and maintenance basis."[2]

Independence and self-government for Tanganyika had to be taken as given. Thus, for purposes of planning, the Colonial government was required to block out progressive stages to achieve a goal that it had not itself determined. Further, the over-all plan for an independent Tanganyika, which was implicit at the war's end, did not postulate a date at which the plan would be realized. The problems of systematically working toward, and preparing for, independence were severely complicated by this variable time factor which in 1948 was thought to be a generation in length, at the shortest. As each step was taken toward realization of independence, the time factor was progressively shortened so that every step toward self-government drastically narrowed the remaining plan-time available. Time is a major variable which planners normally can hold constant, and national development programs generally are labeled three-, five-, or seven-year plans. The phenomenon of planned disengagement with its attendant variable time factor is deserving of more study than it has to date received.

NATION-BUILDING AS PLANNING

An aspect of the process of projecting a desired state of organizational and social being and then systematically taking a series of steps to realize that condition, peculiarly characteristic of the new African states and vividly demonstrated by Tanzania, concerns the distinction between "state" and "nation." We are, surprisingly, still strait-jacketed by our terminology in the social sciences, despite a decade of study of development, modernization, and new nations. We speak of the "new nations," "national planning," and "nationalism." These and other similar terms, with respect to the political process under way in Africa, are inadequate and frequently do more to confuse than explain.[3] The forces moving toward sovereign state status in various arbitrarily defined regions of Africa are hardly comparable to the nationalism that drove Czechs, Serbs, Americans, Hungarians, or Koreans to acquire their own state sovereignty so as to give free reign to a common history, culture, language, or heritage. The *élan* of African "nationalism" is in part a whirlwind set in motion by a bipolar world balance of power. In large part it stems from the black man's long-standing irritation with his subordinate status and the postwar emergence of a world situation conducive to changing it. African nationalism might be usefully regarded as an effort to achieve racial dignity and equality on the coattails of state sovereignty. This distinction is important for the purposes of this study, because if we are to concern ourselves with the ends or purposes of planning in its more restrictive sense, it is important that we clearly comprehend the general goals toward which the plan is implicitly directed. Tanzania is a "state"; it possesses legal sovereignty in that its legal existence has been recognized by the nations of the world and by international organizations. Its independence is not contested. Planned disengagement, which was largely carried out by the British, culminated in the establishment of a sovereign Tanganyikan state. However, Tanzania is not yet a nation, for it does not possess a sense of collective being or identity. As late as 1951 the United Nations Visiting Mission reported a complete lack of a sense of territorial consciousness.[4] What is currently under way in Tanzania may precisely be termed "nation-building"; its development plan may be regarded as state planning for the purposes of constructing a "nation."

Dr. Julius Nyerere, the father of Tanganyikan statehood and the would-be father of Tanzanian nationhood, is acutely aware of this distinction. The prime ministership, he realizes, is an ideal position from which to establish and operate the state. This is not unimportant, particularly when we realize that Tanganyika is dependent for the success of its domestic nation-building upon its capacity to manipulate sources of external assistance. In January 1962, however, Nyerere shocked the leaders of the West, and those of Africa as well, with his decision to resign his prime ministership so as to concentrate his activities in the Tanganyika African National Union (TANU). There exists no sharper illustration of this distinction than Nyerere's realization that though he had succeeded in establishing a "state," the equally important task of building a nation was still to be undertaken and these two tasks required separate though related plans. "It must be realized that Tanganyika is not a nation," he said. "We are trying to build a nation." [5]

A careful observation of the nation-building process in Tanzania and elsewhere in Africa suggests that the purposes or ends toward which planning is directed are twofold and interrelated. The over-all end sought is a state of being conducive to a maximum of human dignity in terms of both a psychological sense of racial pride and equality and a level of material existence consistent with such pride. State sovereignty marks the acquisition of the criteria of equal membership in the world community that establishes eligibility of achievement. Modernization is the term we apply to the process of acquiring the skills and resources necessary to establish a state of physical and psychological well-being commensurate with the over-all goals sought.

NATION-BUILDING AND DEMOCRACY

To be an independent nation-state in the world of today, regardless of which model or combination of competing models is followed, requires that the decisional mechanism required to achieve modernization be accountable ultimately to the will of the people. Even the most authoritarian regimes in our time insist that they rule in the name of the "people." Thus, it is imperative if Tanzania is really to "arrive," really to be "independent," really to be the home of the free and the equal, that a Tanzanian "people" emerge. This is necessary in order to provide the political base or context of national consensus which is required if the system is to operate in a twentieth-century "democratic" fashion. Until very recently national consensus existed only to oust the British and to establish an independent state for the nonnational reasons noted above. Therefore, the decision-makers, in the absence of a fundamental national consensus, are forever threatened by would-be elites who are free to outbid them in an irresponsible manner by employing antinational appeals to gain the mass support that is required to legitimize leadership in newly emergent political systems. Faced with this dilemma, the decision-makers of the new African state, if they are to persist in office, have found it necessary either to "neutralize" this opposition or to manipulate the nonconsenting mass to believe that they, *i.e.*, the existing decision-makers, are in fact delivering the goods of modernization as promised during the independence struggle. It is, of course, impossible for any leadership to deliver the goods according to the plan outlined during the period of disengagement when anti-European and anticolonial agitation served to bid up expectations. The promises made during the era of independence agitation inevitably guarantee that an opposition will arise after independence to challenge the elite's failure to meet the inflated promises. This opposition may take form within the "independence" party or it may be realized in an opposition party.

These symptoms were apparent in Tanganyika within three months after independence. Until the summer of 1962 it seemed as if Julius Nyerere had chosen the difficult path of building national consensus and a national community in a competitive environment in contrast to the alternative of containing or circumscribing the opposition as demonstrated by Kwame Nkrumah in Ghana, Sékou Touré in Guinea, and General Abboud in the Republic of the Sudan. His decision resembled the similar efforts to achieve national unity made famous by Ben-Gurion of Israel and U Nu of Burma. His success or failure will go far to determine the future of democracy and democratic planning in East Africa, and possibly in all of Africa.

In the summer of 1962 Tanganyika, the Cinderella African democracy, reluctantly found it necessary to circumscribe the democratic process in order to protect the embryonic nation from the growing threats of an opposition determined to supplant the existing elite in an undemocratic fashion. Thus, in a classic, though unfortunate, illustration of the dilemma of new nations wherein democracy must be curtailed in order to preclude its destruction, the Tanganyika Legislature in September 1962 passed the Preventive Detention Act. The words of Dr. Nyerere, explaining the controversial act at a press conference, are revealing:

> We cannot be defeated at the ballot box at the moment. There are some realizing this who we have every reason to believe are prepared to use other means. . . . As long as other political

parties campaign on the grounds they have a better policy, this is democracy. But when democratic means are being used to threaten the security of the State, then the normal laws of the Country are inadequate.

The implicit plan is to build a sense of national identity and establish a consensual floor beneath which differences as to what the Tanzania of the future should resemble, and what the best steps to achieve that future may be, may not fall. Nyerere regards TANU as the major instrument in nation-building and is prepared to protect that instrument even at the price of weakening the democratic foundations of the state. At the press conference on the Preventive Detention Act he said: "The only internal cementing force in the country is TANU. Thank God TANU is successful, thank God TANU is peaceful."

However, in 1964 an event occurred which raised considerable doubt about the strength of TANU as the "internal cementing force." The 1964 Army Mutiny is described in detail here, for it demonstrates the inherent political tension within which a new nation must formulate and execute plans.

During the early hours of January 20, 1964, the men of the First Battalion Tanganyikan Rifles began what is now termed a mutiny of the Tanganyikan Army. The mutiny was apparently carried out due to dissatisfaction over pay, promotion, and the fact that expatriate British officers were still in command of the Tanganyikan Rifles. The chain of events began when the soldiers arrested their British officers and the N.C.O.'s at Colito Barracks. Following this action a number of soldiers drove into Dar es Salaam, where they took effective control of the city, seizing the airport and other strategic points. Later in the day, following assurances given by Foreign and Defense Minister Oscar S. Kambona that their demands would be met, the soldiers returned to their barracks.

A smaller scale mutiny occurred in Tabora on January 21, when men of the Second Battalion Tanganyikan Rifles arrested their officers and made essentially the same demands as their counterparts at Colito. These demands were met, too.

On January 25 British Marine Commandos from the aircraft carrier *Centaur* were flown in to both Dar and Tabora. They took complete control of the bases, disarming the mutineers. A short time later Tanganyikan police arrested most of the leaders of the Tanganyika Federation of Labor. President Nyerere in a speech that day said that it had been necessary to disarm the army because it had developed into a force threatening the security of the nation. A new army would be created using members of the TANU Youth League as a nucleus.

British military units remained in Tanganyika until early April, when they were replaced by elements of the Nigerian Army. The replacement was completed by April 10. On May 22 prison sentences of five to fifteen years were handed down to fourteen N.C.O.'s and men of the First Battalion Tanganyikan Rifles.

Since the mutiny, Tanzania has begun the slow process of building a new army. The new army personnel must be members of either TANU, the Afro-Shirazi Party (Zanzibar), or their respective youth wings. Further, the army is now represented in the TANU National Executive.

Comprehensive analysis of planning (national and state) for Tanzania will, of necessity, address itself to the relation of planning to nation-building and to the role of political parties and other quasi-public institutions in the over-all process.

Prior to examining in more detail the planning process in the disengagement and independence phase, it will be useful to sketch briefly the constitutional evolution that culminated in self-government and the establishment of a republic.

POLITICAL AND GOVERNMENTAL TRANSITION

The first signs of African "nationalism" can be traced to 1929 and the establishment of the Tanganyika African Association (TAA), though it was more a social and urban association than a mass political party. The Tanganyika African National Union (TANU), which was really the first political organization of any significance, was founded by Dr. Julius Nyerere in 1954. At that time Nyerere explicitly stated that the purpose of the party was in effect to "plan" for the future. The party's function is that of "preparing the people of Tanganyika for self-government and independence." [6] The distinction between preparation for self-government and the winning of self-government is important and should not be overlooked. Party strength in 1956 was about 100,000, by 1957

it had doubled, and in 1960 it was estimated in excess of 500,000.[7]
Tanganyika's heterogeneous population contains in addition to
its 9,000,000 Africans about 84,000 Asians, 23,000 Arabs, and
approximately 23,000 Europeans. The Europeans, too, had plans
for the country and were organized in the Tanganyika European
Council, an exclusively settler party which maintained close ties
with similar groups in the Rhodesias, Nyasaland, and Kenya. This
group sought to delay constitutional change, which it correctly
concluded would progressively increase the power of the Africans,
and after the 1951 constitutional revisions resolved to "approach
neighboring territories to join in a protest to the British Government." [8]

Tanganyika as a territory was divided for administrative purposes into nine provinces and fifty-five districts. However, after
independence provinces and districts were renamed regions and
areas, respectively. Also, the administrative units have been increased and there are now seventeen regions and fifty-eight areas.
As in most other British dependencies executive authority was
vested in the governor, representing the Crown. In matters of major
policy the governor acted under the direction of the secretary of
state for the colonies. The governor was assisted by an executive
council composed of the senior government officials and a number
of unofficial representatives.

The first Legislative Council, established in 1926, was composed of thirteen official and ten nominated unofficial members.
In practice two of the nominated members represented the Indian
community. One European nominated member was selected to
represent the interests of the African community. In 1945, in recognition of the growing power of the indigenous peoples, the constitution was amended. The unofficial representation was increased
from ten to fourteen—only one less than the reconstituted official
side. The governor appointed the fourteen unofficial members, once
their candidacy had been established through a form of indirect
election. More important, however, was the inclusion of four
Africans in the Legislative Council.

The Executive Council of seven official and four unofficial
members, presided over by the governor, was the effective policy-
making body. The governor's powers were further augmented by
his prerogative of selecting the unofficial members of the Executive
Council.

The budget was traditionally drafted by the financial secretary before it was submitted to the governor and the Executive Council for approval. Once approved, the budget was laid before the Legislative Council.[9] Expenditure estimates were compiled from submissions made by department heads and by the provincial administration. The financial secretary possessed detailed control over these estimates until the introduction of the ministerial system. Under this system ministries were in effect self-accounting and many of the budgeted allocations were made on a ministerial rather than on a project basis. This allowed the minister considerable initiative in framing his departmental budget but considerably diminished the centralized control of the financial secretary's office. The revenue estimates remained the principal responsibility of the financial secretary's office. These estimates were based on the projection of such variables as taxable population and trade statistics. The statistical material available is so meager that great reliance is placed upon historical trends. As a consequence, substantial inaccuracies are not uncommon.

In 1949 the governor appointed a committee of the Legislative Council to consider the need and nature of further constitutional changes. It is at this point that one can detect a preview of the sweeping constitutional changes that the future held in store for Tanganyika. The committee reported—and the governor accepted the view—that a realistic foundation for political development depended upon equal distribution of unofficial seats in the Legislative Council between the three racial communities: African, Asian, and European. The 1951 report of the Constitutional Development Committee in conjunction with a report in 1952 by Professor W. J. M. Mackenzie, a special commissioner appointed to consider the most appropriate system for election to the Legislative Council, led to a further revision of the constitution in 1955, with the result that the Legislative Council was increased from twenty-nine to sixty-one members and the government majority reduced to one. The thirty unofficial members were drawn equally, ten from each major racial group. The Governor's Council—as of this date termed the Executive Council—was increased with the addition of an African and an Asian member to a total of six unofficial members (two from each racial block) and eight official members.

The Tanganyika European Council's position was so inconsistent with this trend of events that it was subsequently replaced by the United Tanganyika Party (UTP) in 1956, which, although accepting the eventuality of ultimate independence and an African government, was considerably more moderate as to how and when this should take place than was the predominantly African TANU. Although UTP posed as a multiracial party, some observers claimed that it owed its support to the government. In the first national elections in 1958/59 every voter cast three ballots in three-seat constituencies for a candidate from each of the three racial communities. In this election UTP was able to elect only one candidate.

The constitution was again altered in December 1959, with the changes providing for the first time an unofficial majority in the Executive Council. It also established fifty constituencies to return seventy-one members, with eleven seats being reserved for Asians and ten for Europeans. Africans won all of the fifty open seats, with the result that the new Legislative Council was composed of fifty elected Africans, ten elected Europeans, eleven elected Asians, plus nine nominated members of whom three were African, two Asian, and one European. In October 1960 responsible government was granted and the Executive Council became the Council of Ministers, with an altered composition giving increased weight to unofficial members and African representatives. Of the eight ministers six were African, one European, and one Asian. In May 1961 the next-to-last step before full independence was heralded by changing the Legislative Council to the National Assembly, the Council of Ministers to the Cabinet, and the Chief Minister to Prime Minister. Complete independence followed on December 9.

Following the pattern established by a number of other former British dependencies, Tanganyika decided after less than six months of independence as a dominion to sever its ties with the Crown and establish a republic. This can best be interpreted as another device to promote the development of a sense of national identity and unity. An official report stated:

> Our nationalism is a young nationalism, born of the desire to unite and free ourselves from the shackles of colonialism. . . . We need to foster our sense of nationhood, and the need to mobilize the physical and spiritual resources of the country in the task of development are inseparable.[10]

The major alteration is the innovation of an executive president. The president is the head of state, commander in chief of the armed forces, and possesses full executive authority. In the exercise of his executive functions, unless otherwise provided by law, he acts on his own discretion. Nor is he bound to accept or seek advice. The president appoints a vice-president and ministers from the National Assembly. The vice-president and ministers presided over by the president comprise the Cabinet. In the elections for the first president on November 1, 1962, Dr. Julius Nyerere, the TANU candidate, won an overwhelming victory.

The significance of this constitutional transition is manifold, but for our purposes particular attention should be drawn to its rapidity and to its chronologically planned sequence. The former has given rise to a series of vexing problems, analyzed below, and the latter has further strengthened a prior inclination to move toward sought-for goals by explicit planned stages.

In April 1964 the governments of Tanganyika and Zanzibar agreed to merge the territories into one united republic. These arrangements have given rise to considerable expansion in government administration. The number of ministries has been increased to nineteen, including a Directorate for Development Planning. The Constitution, too, has been modified; there are now two vice-presidents representing Tanganyika and Zanzibar. Undoubtedly, more adjustments will be made to accommodate the new conditions generated by the merger.

DEVELOPMENT PLANS

Economic growth since 1948 has been substantial, and most authorities estimate the rate of increase of gross national product at about 6.5 per cent annually with a net growth of about 5 per cent. Gross domestic product for 1961 was 187 million pounds and average per capita income in the vicinity of twenty pounds.[11]

This increase is particularly remarkable when it is noted that a government fiscal survey of Kenya, Uganda, and Tanganyika in 1946 seriously questioned Tanganyika's capacity to produce a tax revenue annually of 3.8 to 4.0 million pounds, for "it is not the methods of raising revenue that are lacking in Tanganyika but the liquid wealth from which to raise it." (Tax revenue in 1961/62 was about 17 million pounds.)[12]

The dependency of the economy on sisal exports is long standing and has been most clearly revealed in recent years. Tanganyika provides sisal fiber for some 90 per cent of the world's consumption of baler twine. The decline in world consumption in 1952 after the artificial increase resulting from the Korean War was disastrous and seriously affected the economy. The international coffee and cotton markets are nearly as volatile. In short, the nature of Tanganyika's exports gives them low domestic elasticity of supply to price. Imports, on the other hand, have a low price elasticity. Thus, Tanganyika's economy tends to boom during periods of rising prices for export products and to fall quickly in periods of recession.

A willingness and a readiness to plan the territory's development and economic future was keynoted by Sir Wilfrid Woods in his survey of the economics of the three East African territories:

> There is no real hope . . . of achieving a broader base except by the adoption of active and extensive development measures by the territory's government. A selection of sound plans is one prerequisite of these measures.[13]

The Tanganyika government responded in 1947 by establishing a separate development budget—the first in East Africa. Planning of some consequence, however, had preceded this administrative arrangement, for the Tanganyika Planning Committee, established in 1944, appointed a subcommittee to "consider in fuller detail a number of special problems such as the development of the road system of the country, and the coordination of development proposals in regard to agriculture, animal husbandry and soil conservation." [14]

The 1946 Ten Year Plan made provisions for a capital investment of 10.6 million pounds together with a recurrent expenditure of 7.2 million pounds. The emphasis was on communications, as well it might have been in a large, sparsely populated country whose major productive centers are widely separated and distant from the coast. About 2 million pounds were allocated for the Tanganyika railroad.[15] The 5.2 million pounds allocated for education included provisions for a comprehensive scheme to rehabilitate and train ex-servicemen—recognition on the part of the colonial government of the disruptive potential of these returned veterans. The estimated deficit of 3.3 million pounds was to be covered by refloating outstanding bonds at a lower coupon rate. Before a year had elapsed, however, the plan was altered to include increased educational expenditures.

By 1950 trading conditions had substantially changed and revenue had increased from 6 to 11 million pounds. Furthermore, the railways had ceased to be a responsibility under the plan as a consequence of the establishment of the East African High Commission and its arrangements for independent financing. In addition, private investment in the year 1949 alone is known to have reached as much as 15 million pounds. These tremendous alterations and changes and the tempo of increased economic activity did not leave costs unaffected. In view of these shifting circumstances a revised plan was prepared to cover the years 1950–56 with a projected capital investment of 21.7 million pounds and a recurrent expenditure of 2.7 million, making a total of 24.4 million. The additional finance was to be obtained from the London market (4 million pounds) and the proceeds of the monopoly on cotton marketing (2 million pounds). However, by 1952 development expenditures had already reached nearly 5 million pounds a year and a comparable amount had been spent on the railways by the East African High Commission. Also investment in the groundnut scheme was of substantial proportions and helps explain the rapid rise in revenues, which by 1954 reached 19 million pounds.

The peak of the economic boom in Tanganyika can be dated at this point. Although the decline from this peak did not substantially affect the actual expenditure under the revised plan, real expenditure was considerably less and the number of projects completed fewer than anticipated. An estimate of actual expenditure up to 1954 is about 18 million pounds compared with the 20 million that had been projected.

The abrupt changes which affected the 1946–56 plan in 1952 and 1954 persuaded the government to draft a new plan to commence in 1955. This plan called for expenditures of 25.8 million pounds over the ensuing five years. Two new items were introduced. The government planned to invest 3 million pounds in a central rail link between the northern and southern lines to open up the fertile Kilombero Valley. At the time the plan was drafted the railways were unable to give this project a high enough priority to satisfy Tanganyika, therefore requiring the Tanganyika government to initiate this development project on its own. Secondly, the government proposed to expand electric power by requiring the two private companies to amalgamate and then to invest 2 million pounds in power plants. As in the past, the government relied for capital funds on the Colonial Development Grants (4 million) and the London market (12 million).

A series of reports in 1957 on education, medical services, and agricultural productivity brought about in that year a revision of the 1955–60 plan. The revision called for increasing expenditure by another 10 million pounds, thereby raising the gap between known resources and planned expenditures to nearly 5 million pounds. This underlying optimism was sharply checked the following year when it was apparent that expenditure was going to be considerably in excess of revenue. Recurrent costs of development projects were beginning to place a strain on the budget as were interest charges. A retrenchment of 2 million pounds in capital works was immediately implemented. Despite this sudden jolt, however, the plan was largely completed with financial assistance from Britain, which permitted development expenditure to return from 3 to 6 million pounds.

It is important at this juncture to point out that if one evaluates the planning process in Tanganyika in terms of "planning" in its orthodox sense he would likely conclude that there has been little, if any, real "planning" there. The terms "plan" and "planning" have been appended on numerous occasions to a conglomerate of *ad hoc* schemes and public work projects that would hardly be so dignified in countries where the "plan" is an architectural blueprint and "planning" a professional science.

Responsibility for national planning at the center has traditionally been scattered throughout the relevant ministries in the government. The little coordination that was achieved was primarily a product of a special planning committee within the Cabinet. In mid-1962, however, the minister of finance announced that the government was to establish an economic development commission to consist of a committee of ministers, a coordinating committee of officials, and a secretariat under a director of planning. In December 1962 the president, in his opening address to Parliament, stated that he planned to set up a department of development planning "directly under my control."

A characteristic of colonial administration was the annual report required from each district from the senior representatives of the various departments and administration. To the harried administrators or technicians, preparation of the annual report has tended to be an unwelcome task, made somewhat easier by altering last year's report with current statistics and similarly worded recommendations. It is not surprising, therefore, that Tanganyika's development plans more often than not have comprised the amalgamation and subsequent ministerial pruning of local projects and proposals, some of which had been repeated year after year. The systematic "planning" that has occurred has tended to be of an *ad hoc,* special purpose nature. For example, all three East African territories have invested considerable resources and plans in such areas as "community development," "local government," and "Agriculture." Rarely, however, have these *ad hoc* plans been coordinated and considered in terms of a single national plan. "Planning" traditionally has been perceived in East Africa more as a frame of mind or general approach than as precise methodology, which has characterized the process in India and the Soviet Union.

Contrary to the recommendations of the World Bank, the Tanganyika government's 1961–64 development plan called for expenditures of twenty-four million pounds over a three-year period.[16] The success of the earlier two plans has emboldened the government to take a calculated risk on more funds being available upon independence. The 1961–64 plan called for capital expenditure of twenty-four million pounds, of which the largest item is for education (13.8 per cent) followed closely by trunk roads (13.5 per cent).

In its most recent plan (1964–69) the Tanzania government calls for expenditures of 246 million pounds over a five-year period. The public sector is expected to contribute 130 million pounds, of which the central government's contribution is 102 million pounds. The plan stresses the development of social infrastructure (mainly education) which is to receive 28.4 per cent of the central government expenditures and agricultural development which is to receive 27.1 per cent of the central government's contribution. In the five-year period the private sector is expected to contribute 116 million pounds toward development. Thirty-one per cent of this amount is expected to be directed to industrial development.[17]

National planning, to the extent to which it can be said to have existed in Tanganyika, was the responsibility, until 1962, of a Cabinet committee composed of the functional ministers and selected officials under the chairmanship of the prime minister. In the spring of 1962, however, the government established the Economic Development Commission (EDC), which included a ministerial committee, a coordinating committee, and a planning secretariat. The composition of the ministerial committee of the EDC generally resembles that of its predecessor. Added, however, are arrangements for a coordinating committee composed of the permanent secretaries of the constituent ministries of the EDC. Also authorized in the current scheme is a planning secretariat divided into two sections—planning and plan implementation. The secretariat is to consist of a director of planning (of permanent secretary rank), a principal assistant secretary (in charge of plan implementation), an assistant secretary, and two economists.

In effect the EDC is the national planning commission and the two titles in practice are synonymous. In April 1964 further reorganization of government agencies occurred. Under these arrangements—necessitated in part by the Tanganyika-Zanzibar merger—the total number of ministries as noted was increased to nineteen. Some of the former ministries, including the Ministry of Development Planning, were dissolved and a new agency, the Directorate of Development Planning, was established. The directorate was charged with all matters relating to future national development. However, all policy matters continued to be considered for approval by the Economic Development Commission. In this respect the directorate might be regarded as the technical advisor to the main political agency concerned with national development, i.e., the Economic Development Commission. Also, a new ministry responsible for lands, settlements, and water development was established, with one of its primary functions being the implementation of the village settlement policy. This reorganization further emphasizes the importance attached to the development of rural areas through a village settlement policy.

The eventual role of the planning secretariat, vis-à-vis the planning staff and activities of the separate ministries, will likely be determined in large part by the skill and philosophy that the director of planning brings to the office. There is within government considerable admiration for the French approach to national planning. This, when added to the appointment of a French director of planning, may be indicative of the direction that future organization and activities will take.

The 1961/62–1963/64 development plan contributed to the establishment, in 1962, of two new planning and development institutions. The Tanganyika Development Corporation is a wholly government-owned public body designed to stimulate industrial and mineral development through strategic investment of public funds. It commenced operations early in 1963 with an initial share capital of 500,000 pounds. The director of the Tanganyika Development Corporation reports directly to the Ministry of Commerce and Industry. Generally the TDC, like similar institutions in other countries, provides a channel whereby government funds and organization can be employed to finance, and if necessary manage, industrial enterprise critical to national development but not sufficiently attractive to private investment.[18]

The Tanganyika Development Company, unlike the development corporation, is a joint venture involving at its initiation the participation of the TDC, the Commonwealth Development Corporation (formerly known as the Colonial Development Corporation), and the West German Development Bank. Policy-making, provision of capital, and management of the company are shared among the three participating institutions. The initial share capital of 1.5 million pounds was provided in equal parts by the Tanganyika Development Corporation, an agency of the Federal Republic of Germany, and the Commonwealth Development Corporation. Provision exists for inviting other domestic and foreign participants, and there is some indication that other sources of external cooperation will be forthcoming. For example, the Netherlands Overseas Finance Corporation and the International Finance Company have both expressed interest in joining the venture.[19]

The establishment of TDC and the development company, as well as the commercial advisory division and the industrial development division of the Ministry of Commerce and Industry is based largely on the *World Bank Report* and a study of the bases for the expansion of industrial processing activities undertaken for Tanganyika by Arthur D. Little, Inc.[20]

The most recent plan (1964–69) emphasizes the reliance on

external capital resources. In its financial provisions, 128.5 million
pounds or 52.4 per cent of the estimated total capital investment
is to be obtained from nondomestic sources.

The international nature of development planning in Tanganyika is further indicated by this demonstrated willingness to ignore
the World Bank recommendations. So long as the greater part of
the resources to meet the development plan's needs are obtained
from abroad, there is little need to be limited by an assessment of
purely local resources. For in this situation it is not local resources
that determine the level of development (or for that matter even
the nature of development) but rather a capacity to attract external
assistance. Little is known about what we might term the international gamesmanship of planning. In theory there is no limit to
the resources Tanganyika can attract from abroad. Thus, the development plan and budget become a ploy in the game. Therefore,
while independence has removed one of the floating variables that
traditionally retarded the planning process (the independence date
as a time variable), it has added another variable that can vary
independently from the domestic Tanganyika decisional process.
It is partly for this reason that the planning process continues to
be uncertain, and less an explicit reconciliation of available resources to a development program than it is a token in the international development sweepstakes. The 1962/63 capital budget
estimates classified nearly 3 million of the 8.3 million pounds anticipated capital expenditures as "deficit to be found from external
sources." [21] As noted, the current five-year plan expects 52.4 per
cent of its estimated total capital requirements to be raised from
external sources.

"Do the skills required to allocate capital investment of this magnitude efficiently exist in Tanzania?" some observers ask. The
short fall of over one million pounds in anticipated capital expenditures in 1961/62 was "caused mainly by a lack of capacity and
qualified staff to carry out the various projects." [22] The philosophy
of administration underlying colonial rule was based upon a belief
in the superior capacity of the nonspecialized administrative officer
to formulate and administer successfully whatever policy the situation demanded. A legacy of the intuitive generalist, with an accompanying tendency to deprecate the specialist, lingers in Tanganyika
as it does elsewhere in British and former British Africa and is

often perpetuated by the expatriate former colonial officials who continue to hold strategic administrative positions. Thus, whereas "planning" is viewed as necessary and even desirable, it is often felt that planners and similar specialists are not really essential. An editorial statement in a newly established Tanganyika journal reinforces the point:

> It is essential if these plans and intentions are to be carried out, to set up adequate planning machinery. Amidst the myriads of experts coming to Tanganyika the importation of a few planning experts could act as the leaven to the economy. The aid, both financial and in manpower that Tanganyika is receiving or has been promised is quite considerable—but can she utilize it?
>
> Last year's estimated expenditure on development was not used due to the lack of planning machinery.
>
> Dr. Nyerere has stated that one of the most urgent needs of independence is a decolonizing of the mind. Nowhere is this truer than in the economic field.[23]

An interesting addition to the three-year plan (1961–64), which reflects the independent status of Tanganyika and also the new costs and requirements for development inherent in independence, is a category termed "the Prime Minister's Office," for which slightly more than 1,000,000 pounds of the development plan are allocated.

> With that amount it is hoped that it will be possible to meet the inescapable commitments of Tanganyika's forthcoming independence which fall within the portfolio of the Prime Minister: to continue the present program for the construction of new government offices in Dar es Salaam; to provide for the reorganization of the provincial administration by expanding the Administrative Training Center at Mzumbe, and by constructing new offices and extending existing offices in the field; to complete the construction of office accommodations for honorable members of the National Assembly; and to absorb the capital works projects of the former Ministry of Information Services in respect of information services, the government press and broadcasting.[24]

This item also includes 240,000 pounds for the establishment of embassies.

Obviously Tanzania must rely on external financial assistance for its development and for the success of its plan, as it has in the past. When the United States on the date of Tanganyikan Independence presented the new nation with a long-term, low-rate loan of ten million dollars, West Germany announced that it would provide a comparable sum.

This survey of the manner in which men of mixed motive, color, and nationality have sought to reshape the lands and peoples of Tanganyika so as to "improve" their physical and psychological well-being raises two general points: (a) the assumption that national development and planning must be based primarily upon large-scale development of peasant agriculture, and (b) the question of the dialectics of scale whereby development and planning depend on the one hand upon the systematic procurement of international human and physical resources but on the other hand upon massive alterations in human behavior and beliefs and upon related procurement of mass consent, which in turn depends upon the contribution of local institutions and leadership.

We shall conclude this preliminary survey of national planning in Tanganyika with a more detailed examination of these two general questions.

National Development and Peasant Agriculture

The failure of the groundnut plan ironically has discouraged other large-scale agricultural schemes, but at the same time the remnants of the groundnut program have given rise to a number of middle-scale planned farming enterprises which neither have won the support of the Tanganyikan peasant nor have proven economically sound. Elspeth Huxley may have stated the case a bit strongly, but her view that "a modern state with its expensive social services, can no more be built on a basis of peasant agriculture than a skyscraper could be built of mud blocks on a potato patch," should give cause not necessarily to reject but constantly to re-examine the assumption that concentration on peasant agriculture is the "bootstrap" of nation-building.[25]

One wonders whether the soil, rainfall, and transport system of Tanzania will ever enable the profitable, unsubsidized marketing of an agricultural surplus in competition with the abundance and even surplus of primary foodstuffs produced in the more strategically located and better endowed regions of the world. This writer is not an economist and therefore may be permitted to raise this simple, but fundamental, question. Urged on by postwar planning initiated in a food-scarce United Kingdom, augmented by the East African Royal Commission Report of 1955, sanctified by the excellent World Bank study and report of 1960, and given implementation by successive national development plans, Tanzania, a poorly endowed land mass, is being propelled along a path demanding an increasingly heavy sacrifice on the part of the people plus massive external capital assistance so as to become a primary producer and exporter of foodstuffs.

Of the eighteen million pounds of capital expenditure recommended by the *World Bank Report,* nearly one-sixth is allocated for water development to enable Tanzania to build the peasant agricultural economy that is assumed requisite to development. If we add to this the amounts recommended for agricultural settlement schemes, veterinary medicine needs, and loans to TAC, the portion of over-all capital development allocated generally for agricultural improvement is in excess of 25 per cent of the total.[26] The actual development plan for 1961/62–1963/64 allocated nearly one-third of 23,930 pounds—the three-year plan capital expenditure—for agriculture, veterinary medicine, forestry, water supply and irrigation, TAC, and cooperative development. In contrast only about 4 per cent of the capital of the total development plan has been allocated for the development corporation, industrial credit, geological mapping, and mineral surveys. The two remaining items of significance in the development plan are education, 13.8 per cent, and trunk roads, 13.5 per cent. (In one respect even the extension of trunk roads is directed toward the development of peasant agriculture.)[27]

Similarly the current (1964–69) plan emphasizes the development of rural areas. Eleven per cent of the total expenditure of 246 million pounds is directed to agricultural improvement. In addition many of the other major items of expenditure, including education, trunk and feeder roads, and health are directed toward rural development. In fact, 40 per cent of the total capital expenditures would be a conservative estimate of the amount directed to rural de-velopment.

Is this over-all planning philosophy of turning Tanganyika into a major primary producer of foodstuffs, despite the reluctance of both the land and the people to be a party to the scheme, the only path to national development? Our purpose here is not to answer this query but simply to raise it. Existing knowledge of the limita-tions of physical resources of Tanzania relative to agricultural production and the necessity of costly development of water re-sources would seem to this noneconomist to raise the question of possible alternative or parallel paths to national development. It may well be that there are none or that an agricultural revolution must come first, but this likelihood is a factor that should be defi-nitely determined before plans are implemented based on the as-sumption that the development of peasant agriculture is the sole avenue to modernity.

Sir Ernest Vasey, who made an extraordinary contribution to the economic development of Tanganyika, strongly supports the orthodox view, noting that as nearly half of the country's total money income is derived from export and that about four-fifths of export earnings are attributable to agricultural and livestock products, "the task of securing wide-spread income increase in the present stage is one of agricultural and livestock develop-ment." [28]

The emphasis upon commercial-exportable agricultural devel-opment is not unanimous even in Tanzania. Dr. W. Kalpish, one-time development adviser to the government, questioned the long-run implications of this philosophy. "Even assuming a five-fold increase in agricultural production (and assuming at that that this could physically be done, which I doubt), the per capita income would still be in the vicinity of say sixty to eighty pounds per capita, which would be excellent in the context of present figures but still miserably low compared to the per capita income of industrialized countries." [29] Kalpish has also raised the question we have noted above. Given the world market and a surplus agricultural produc-tive capacity, where would Tanganyika sell its five-fold increase in agricultural exports? As he points out, "there is at present an international coffee agreement for the purpose not of increasing, but limiting production to what the world can take." [30]

Surely planned increases in the production of agricultural food-stuffs can be defended on the basis of increasing domestic consumption and variety as an investment in human resources. It also might be employed to increase the nonfarm proportion of the labor market as a preliminary step toward industrialization. But, Kalpish believes, "it certainly is not the final answer to achieve the purpose of development, namely a sound, balanced economy with its own impetus to sustain further development in which people can work and live decently."[31]

Dialectic of Scale

> The majority of the people remained unconvinced of need for soil conservation and other measures, and were resentful of the extra work involved in carrying them out.[32]

Rural societies in Africa, possibly even more so than in most other developing regions of the world, are peculiarly parochial. The predominant characteristic of the traditional forms of social and political organization, with some notable exceptions, has been their small-scale and parochial nature. This near anarchistic kinship-type pluralism, through the centuries, has given rise to an extraordinary and tenacious value investment on the part of thousands of distinct communities for doing certain things in established ways. This smallness of scale in conjunction with organizational diffusion renders the various aspects of the traditional sociopolitical system peculiarly interdependent. It is hardly possible, therefore, regardless of the clarity and logic of a national plan, to alter only selected aspects of traditional behavior and to leave others intact.

The African population of Tanganyika is divided into approximately 125 distinct tribal groupings varying in population from nearly a million in the case of the Sukuma to as few as 3,000 or 4,000 for some of the smaller tribes. It is possible to speak of Tanganyika as a "multi-nation state" and of the process of nation-building as an effort to develop a sense of common, overarching nationality. National planning, from this point of view, can be treated as a rational attempt to develop those conditions within the *state* of Tanzania that are conducive to the emergence of a Tanzanian *nation*. This requires on the one hand the involvement of

this multitude of distinct communities in an associational life that
transcends traditional localities. The politics of the period of disengagement in Tanganyika which gave rise to TANU and to large-
scale political activity were among the first steps in building a sense
of Tanganyikan national identity in the masses. It also acted to
educate them as to the indignity of their subordinate status, to
bring to them an awareness of the possibility of an improved
physical existence, and to inform them of the promises of the party
enough to create a demand for the meeting of expectations by an
independent national government.

Those who now seek to build a Tanzanian nation must meet the
expectations of the masses which they themselves were responsible
for raising in the process of securing self-government. Thus, planning the economic and social welfare development of the country
is a political necessity if statehood is to lead to nationhood and if
those now holding positions of political influence are not to be
replaced. In 1960 Nyerere said: "We find that our country must
learn to think as a nation, and we are faced with the question of
organization and of getting the 120 tribes to think of themselves as
one people." [33]

The three-year development plan and the current five-year plan
both reflect a systematic effort to deliver on the campaign promises
of the struggle for independence. Independence for Tanganyika
required little alteration in the day-to-day behavior and beliefs of
the masses of men and women inhabiting the country. However, if
the promises inherent in independence are to be met, far-reaching
alterations in human behavior, loyalties, and beliefs are required.
The new government is faced with the dilemma of jeopardizing its
support by requiring the members of a hundred or more constituent
traditional communities to change profoundly their ways of life and
beliefs, which have been firmly institutionalized and legitimized
by the parochial institution of nation-tribe. Indirect rule, in the
classical sense, never existed throughout most of Tanganyika. The
ruthlessness of the early German direct administration plus the
indigenous small-scale nature of society and governance in traditional Tanganyika led to what was, in effect, in most areas, direct
rule through a hierarchy of civil service chiefs responsible, not to
the local constituency, but to the British Colonial administration.
This made it generally unnecessary to secure local consent prior

to implementing central policy at the community level. Obviously it is impossible to rule a large territory and population with an extremely small administrative staff, as did the British, without a degree of local consent. The successful administrator rarely sought to implement policy that he knew would conflict radically with the community's desires or values. Nevertheless, the colonial system was in essence authoritarian and alterations in vocational behavior, community life, and values were achieved during the British rule more through (nonphysical) coercion than by a response to locality interest.

Independence—*Uhuru*—has been interpreted as more than the substitution of one flag for another or of a black for a white district commissioner. The philosophy of self government, as well as the withdrawal of the technically superior coercive power of British arms, requires that the masses in Tanzania—more properly the hundreds of communities—give their consent, implicitly if not explicitly, to demands for alterations in their behavior or beliefs.

We would suggest that it is only the local institutions that are capable of processing and translating central policy into directives that will meaningfully alter the behavior of Tanzania's millions in the directions envisaged by a national plan and by the national leaders. This follows, not only because it is only local leadership and institutions that can fill the role of policy broker, but more important it is only they who know the limits beyond which community credibility cannot be stretched and the extent to which new knowledge is actually relevant to altering traditional procedural and substantive values. Agricultural regulations as to what to plant and harvest, where, and at what time, and then when to market, during the colonial area were based primarily upon compulsion. But after independence, these demands for conformity with external decisions must of necessity depend more upon consent and less and less upon coercion. It is not the purpose of this survey to study in detail the critical role of the many institutions of local governance in the process of giving substance and meaning to national planning but only to draw attention to this frequently neglected factor.

Independence, in an important sense, implies decentralization of the power to govern because it requires the procurement of a higher degree of local consent than was formerly the case. Independence tends also to raise immediately the sights and goals of centrally directed development. These two tendencies are not necessarily inconsistent but are conflict-laden and characterize planning in the immediate postindependence state.

In 1959 it was apparent that compulsion was relatively ineffective in securing local compliance with central agricultural regulations in Tanganyika. "Continued enforcement of regulations was impractical without adequate cooperation of the people, and repeal of the regulations . . . followed." [34]

The growing importance of *community development* as a factor in the implementation of national plans is but indicative of the "turnstile" role of local institutions. The goals of community development are popular approval and support for the measures it hopes to promote. However, community development, even though focused on the locality, is often perceived as an external and alien factor. Independence is liable therefore to bring a decline in the role of the central government Department of Community Development and an increased role for the rapidly developing all-purpose local governments.

One of the implications of this point of view is that the real politics of development take place not at the capital city but at the locality level. In the single-party political system that characterizes many new nations, there is little disagreement as to the amount and purposes of planning. It is at the level of the locality that the politics of obtaining consent, of maneuvering for support, of balancing responsibility with authority takes place. The local agricultural officer, for example, if he is to succeed in increasing the yield of peasant cotton farming in Area X, must have the support of the person or institution whose authority the community accepts. [35] The chief has long been the recipient of this legitimacy because he knew who was and who was not influential in the community and under what circumstances influence could be exerted. He knew what could and what could not be done to alter behavior to improve cotton production or marketing. He was also, however, dependent for his promotion on central government administration and had to balance these factors against the necessity of working within a local political framework. It is the politics of accountability and consent-building that lies at the heart of the process of implementing the national plan in Tanganyika. Nor is this matter as simple as the relation of traditional social and political forms to the process of modernization. The local governance institutions, which "turnstile" development to the people in one direction and feed consent to the national decision-makers in the other, vary from one era to another. In Tanganyika, at the present time, three modern local institutions—the political party, the cooperative societies, and the village development committees—are of particular significance in this regard.

The origin and scope of TANU were described above and require no further elaboration here. The resignation of Julius Nyerere from the prime ministership three months after independence mystified many observers of the Tanganyikan scene. It is difficult to believe that a successful political leader would step down from the position of chief of state in order to devote full time to party leadership. But this is in fact what Nyerere did and for reasons that are pertinent to this thesis. In Tanganyika the party had successfully penetrated the thousands of parochial communities and had effectively begun to extend the tribal and village frame of reference to include a sense of association in a Tanganyikan nation. More important, the party organization at the local level, in the absence of highly developed local government, is the key institution capable of processing and translating "state" policy into meaningful alterations in mass behavior. It is the party generally, but more specifically its local branches and organization, that is best equipped and most likely to change Tanzania from a multination state to a unination state. Nyerere knows this better than anyone else, as the following statement illustrates:

> To achieve this objective, Tanganyika needs not only an able elected government, the full support and cooperation of the people, but also a strong political organization active in every village acting like a two-way all-weather road along which the purposes, plans and problems of the government can travel to the people, and ideas, desires and misunderstandings of the people can travel direct to the government. This is the job of the new TANU.[36]

Modern institutions of local governance such as local cooperative societies, political party branches, local government and village development committees are playing an increasingly important role in stimulating development at the local level. The leaders of these new associations are almost without exception relatively young, well-educated men who are closely identified with TANU. The party serves as their link with the center, and their local legitimacy—both traditional and modern—enables them to translate administrative aspects of the national plan into meaningful behavior.

The agricultural "producer cooperatives," as encouraged and superimposed over a peasant agriculture by British Colonial administration, in some respects are the economic counterparts of indirect rule. The small-scale pluralistic units of production could not be individually controlled, coordinated, and marketed. The cooperative as a device was employed in Tanganyika even before the First World War, and by 1939 the Kilimanjaro Native Cooperative Union was already composed of 27 primary cooperative societies with 25,728 members.[37] In 1962, 800 registered societies with a membership of 327,000 united to form the Cooperative Union of Tanganyika. The 1961–64 development plan has allocated 265,000 pounds to cooperative development, including a cooperative college.[38]

The current five-year plan envisages an expansion of the cooperative movement to cover 10 per cent of the value of retail and wholesale consumer trade. Under the provisions of the plan, 7 million pounds is the expected capital expenditure to be designated for expanding cooperative projects by 1970.

Cooperative societies play a major role in the production of cash crops in Tanganyika. The value of cooperative production in 1959 was 11.5 million pounds and accounted for approximately one-quarter of all of Tanganyika's exports.[39] The rate of increase, too, is impressive, and no doubt we have yet to feel the full weight of these societies on the political and economic scales. In 1959 alone 72 new primary societies were registered in Tanganyika.[40] In 1963 there were 100 cooperative officers and inspectors from the central government Department of Cooperative Development in the field. Cooperation looms large in the life of Tanganyika; schools to train cooperative officers and officials have been established, and a central cooperative bank is being planned. In 1962 the government launched a major program to develop consumer cooperatives.

There seems to be no limit to the range of potential activities that might engage the attention and resources of the growing cooperatives. The Kilimanjaro Native Cooperative Union, for example, is today as much concerned with the development and improvement of coffee yield and quality as with its marketing. It operates one of the largest educational enterprises in Tanganyika where it trains a wide range of persons not only in the technique of coffee growing, marketing, etc., but in the science of cooperative management as well. The KNCU is more than an economic institution in the lives of the Chagga. It is composed of 53 societies with a total membership of more than 45,000 farmers cultivating approximately 34,000 acres of coffee.[41] Its Moshi Community Center contains a library, a board room, offices, shops, a modern hotel, a roof garden, a canteen, a laundry, and a restaurant seating 250.[42]

Of more significance than the cooperative's turnstiling of development to the locality are their overlapping interdependent relations with other key institutions of local governance—both modern and traditional. Taken together these local institutions exercising authority over various aspects of communal life are instrumental in changing a national plan from an academic exercise, or a gleam in the eyes of the national planners, to actual alterations in the work-a-day lives of millions of persons. The modern locality institutions are particularly important on this point, because, though membership and leadership are local, they exist as segments in a national association. Thus, local chapters, societies, and party units are the new critical links between traditional parochialism and evolving cosmopolitan nationalism. Without them a plan would remain, but a plan and an intensive study of national planning in Tanganyika must of necessity concentrate its energies on these key strategically placed institutions.

Whereas there has been considerable delay and some confusion over the establishment of government institutions and organization at the capital to carry through the implementation of development plans, considerable organization and activity have occurred at the local level. The Tanganyika government has made a fundamental, and possibly crucial, decision to risk considerable organizational and physical resources on development at the local level.

Instructions went out from the capital during the summer of

1962 to regional and area commissioners to supervise the organization of comprehensive developmental schemes at the local level. Initiation and responsibility for this broad policy is now shared by the president's office, the Ministry of Local Government, the Ministry of Commerce and Cooperatives, and the Ministry of Community and National Culture Development.[43] Ideally, the scheme calls for the establishment of rural village development committees (VDC) and urban ward development committees, in every village and ward in the country. The VDC's, composed of one or two men and women from each nuclear village or hamlet, report their needs to the community development or other local field assistant. The request for financial assistance, or for materials to make possible the completion of a village school, road, community center, or well, is passed, along with accompanying comments, to the District Council and on to the area commissioner, who theoretically brings all requests to a meeting of the Area Development Committee which he himself chairs. The Area Development Committee consists of the area (former district) level representatives of the local ministries, the chief executive officer of the District Council, the area chairman, representatives of TANU, cooperative leaders, the local member of Parliament, and on occasion representatives of other voluntary agencies. The significant point to note, however, is that the organizational chart, correspondence, and circulars specify TANU representation, not simply representatives of "political parties," on the village, area, and regional development committees. The regional commissioners receive funds from the central government for allocation to the constituent areas for self-help schemes to be subsequently distributed and accounted for through the agency of the local government treasury. The scheme is tied to the center through regional development committees, the Ministry of Commerce and Cooperatives, the Ministry of Community Development and National Culture, and a coordinating development committee at the Cabinet level. The significance of "self-help" through the agency of a thousand-plus village development committees, is the manner in which hundreds of thousands of parochially oriented persons are being involved in an organization and in activities directed toward *national* development. Tanganyika's self-help schemes have undergone some rather caustic criticism, much of which certainly is warranted. There have been a number of cases of wasted energy and materials. The village TANU headquarters, which is in an increasing number of villages and serves as a community center, literacy classroom, and the meeting place of the VDC, is the sparkplug of the self-help schemes. There have been instances when TANU enthusiasm has substituted coercion for voluntary "self-help," and when self-help roads were built at an impossible gradient, or when schools and dispensaries were constructed for which staff was not available.

The real significance of the self-help scheme and the organizational pyramid upon which the scheme depends must not, however, be judged solely, or even primarily, upon the number and quality of roads constructed, wells dug, or schools built. As we emphasized earlier, nation-building requires above all the development of a sense of national identity and obligation. This must be planned for and implemented. The village development committees, in some areas at least, are rapidly evolving as the major authoritative institution at the village level. The VDC chairman is almost invariably the local TANU leader. The committee members usually contain a sprinkling of older, traditionally respected individuals, TANU youth leaders, cooperative society chairmen, church leaders, and others.

Of related importance is the abolition of the role and institution of "chief." Divisional executive officers responsible to the chief executive officer of the district council have replaced the traditional or quasi-traditional chiefs in every district and subdistrict in Tanganyika. This innovation is a revolution of major proportions, and the fact that it has been carried out with relatively little friction is a credit to both TANU organization and the cooperation between TANU and the district councils. The "headmen" (subchiefs) who were formerly selected by the chiefs to exercise authority over the village (lowest level in the administrative hierarchy) are today elected. As a consequence the headmen tend to be either local TANU leaders or strongly endorsed by the local TANU branch. Their exofficio presence on the village development committees, and their role in recruiting mass labor for self-help schemes, of course are critical to the success of the entire venture.

New leadership and accompanying institutions are quickly replacing traditional and parochial organizations throughout much of Tanganyika. Legitimacy is notably shifting from the elder, chief, appointed headman, and representatives of the central bureaucracy to the young men who dominate the new democratic district councils, village development committees, and TANU.

The problems of harnessing and integrating the thousands of minor self-help schemes throughout a developing country characterized by a rudimentary communications system are formidable indeed. Attempts have been made to develop reporting schemes and to relate the self-help program to the national development plans. An attempt, not altogether successful, was made to break the three-year development plan into constituent regional programs. This scheme has been abandoned in the current five-year plan. Each village development committee is "requested" to report its production targets in agricultural produce, miles of road to be constructed, number of wells to be dug. For example, after the Area Development Committee formulated estimates for the number of acres of crops to be planted and miles of roads to be built in a given area, each constituent village development committee was assigned proportional targets. One village chosen randomly with approximately 375 taxpayers was required to plant six acres of various crops per taxpayer, cultivate a communal farm of about ten acres, dig two wells, and build a five-mile road.

There is about these new forms of organization and activity a democratic and dynamic element that was absent in the former colonial system. Whereas colonial rule through chiefs and handpicked councils was basically authoritarian, the system currently evolving has some totalitarian aspects. The experiment under way is as fascinating as it is critical for Tanganyika's development. The country's leaders are promoting massive self-help schemes organized through a pyramid of local development committees in cooperation with a rejuvenated local government system—coordinated and coerced where necessary by an all-embracing TANU. This experiment is designed not only to make a major contribution to economic development and welfare, but more important, is expected to alter radically the nature of local legitimacy. Tanganyika's thousands of villages and millions of villagers are to be connected to the national grid via the TANU—Self-Help circuit.

A new term, indicative of the emphasis placed on the role of local institutions in national development, is currently much in vogue. Through the Village Settlement Association (VSA), a fundamental policy close to President Nyerere's heart, "villagization," was launched in 1963. The President, whose knowledge of the country and its people reflects the years he has devoted to party organization and activity, is firmly convinced that the expectations of the masses can be met only if the people are relocated into sizable integrated villages. If local consensus and participation in nation-building are to be forthcoming, it is imperative that TANU and the government be able to communicate with the masses. This can be accomplished, it is thought, only if the population is concentrated in relatively compact villages. The consolidation of land, which of necessity will accompany this bold scheme, will contribute to increased agricultural productivity.

The initial intention of the Tanganyika government was to develop a series of "pilot" settlement projects to serve as experimental stations for future development. Acting on the advice of foreign experts, the government selected eight sites—to be under continuous observation for five or six years—in different parts of the country. However, because of the political urgency felt by the government, the policy has been reoriented to proceed as rapidly as possible—within the limitations of available funds—with the establishment of the maximum number of planned villages.

To date only five schemes have been planned. Of these, three are functioning, one has been started but because of the recent heavy rains work on it was temporarily postponed, and the remaining one has only recently been launched. Although the recommendations of the foreign experts emphasized that the location of villages be primarily determined by economic and technical considerations, it is evident that in Tanganyika political considerations have received priority. The efforts of the commissioner for the VsA to get away from the concept of distributing villages by political regions have not been very successful. Such has been the progress of the village settlement scheme since the policy's public announcement on December 10, 1962.

Few will deny the desirability of redistribution and consolidation of the problematically scattered population of Tanzania. However, there are more than a few observers who question whether this bold experiment is possible, short of a degree of coercion sufficient to deny the very ends sought.

It is ironic that the key to successful nation-building for Tanzania lies not at the level of the state but on the one hand at the level of the locality and on the other hand at the suprastate level. It was noted earlier in this work that "national" planning for a country like Tanzania is a fiction, for those who would plan for Tanzania must concentrate at one and the same time on the local and the international communities.

As a British dependency, Tanzania's future has depended in large part upon British plans for East Africa generally. Except for twenty years or so of German rule and its first year of independence, the land mass and peoples termed Tanganyika have always existed as a ward of the international community—first of the League of Nations and more recently of the United Nations.

Tanzania, though a republic, remains a member of the Commonwealth. Therefore, her continued dependence upon the Sterling Area and upon Commonwealth preference are also international factors that must be considered in the process and politics of "national" planning. More recently the possibilities of British membership in the common market and the economic and political implications of associate membership for Tanzania have come to complicate the planning process. Between 1946 and 1961 the United Kingdom's Colonial Development and Welfare funds channeled a total of more than fifteen million pounds into development schemes in Tanganyika. In addition Tanganyika profited from the sixteen million pounds that were made available to East African regional schemes.[44] Obviously, if this source of assistance were to dry up, as well it might if the United Kingdom were to join the common market and Tanzania were to decide against associate membership as Vice-President Kawawa has indicated she will, and not be replaced by some other external source, Tanzania could not exist as a viable nation-state. Tanzania's new planners are perfectly aware of this and also of the existence of other sources of external assistance, which were not available prior to independence. The politics of planning for Tanzania, therefore, is in its very nature an aspect of Tanzania's international relations and of international politics generally. Negotiations for support, the scope and nature of subsequent accountability, the balancing of competing interest at the international level—these are aspects of the politics of planning which, as we noted above, have their counterpart at the parochial community level.

Development for Tanzania will not occur unless massive external international assistance is obtained and unless institutions of local governance translate plans into action and secure the required degree of mass consent. The politics and critical processes of the over-all development planning program for Tanzania, and probably for other African nations at similar stages of development, occur at these two polar points. A future comprehensive survey and analysis of the process and politics of national planning in Tanzania might well begin by formulating a model built about this dialectic of scale.

Appendix I

Chronology of Planning

1937	Establishment of Central Development Committee
1940	Report of Central Development Committee
1940	Colonial Development and Welfare Act
1943	Reconsideration of Central Development Committee Report
1944	Postwar Development Proposal
1946	Establishment of Development Commission
1946/47	Ten Year (£17.8 million) Development and Welfare Plan for Tanganyika
1947	Development Budget
1950	Revision of 1946/47 Plan to Cover 1950–56 (£24.4 million)
1953–55	East African Royal Commission Study and Report
1955	Five Year Development Plan Based on Report of Royal Commission (£25.8 million)
1957	Reports of Surveys of Education, Agriculture, and Medical Services
1957	Revision of 1955 Plan Based on Reports (£26 million)

	(£ million)
Development of Natural Resources	5.0
Communications	7.5
Urban Development	3.2
Electricity	2.0
Medical	1.4
Education	3.8
Public Buildings	2.0
Urban Housing	1.0

1959	Economic Survey Mission—International Bank for Reconstruction and Development (World Bank)
1960	World Bank Report—Recommends Development Plan (£18 million)
1961	1961–64 Development Plan (£24 million)
1964	1964–69 Economic and Social Development Plan (£246 million)

77

Appendix II

Economic Sectors

A. SUMMARY OF 1961–64 DEVELOPMENT PLAN

Item	£ 000	Per Cent
Prime Minister	1,252	5.2
Agriculture	5,737	24.0
Communications, Power and Works	6,900	28.8
Education	3,270	13.7
Commerce and Industry	1,095	4.6
Local Government	1,244	5.2
Home Affairs	2,180	9.1
Health and Labour	954	4.0
Lands and Surveys	1,298	5.4
Total:	23,930	100.0

1962: Development Commission established responsible for planning to the Cabinet. The prime minister is chairman of the commission, and the finance minister is vice-chairman.

Source: Tanganyika Five Year Plan for Economic and Social Development, 1 July, 1964–30 June, 1969.

B. GROSS CAPITAL FORMATION BY THE

July 1964 to

	Agriculture		Central	
	Irrig. & Resett.	Tradi- tional	Indus- try	Com- merce
1. Agriculture and livestock	10,373	6,886		
2. Forestry		923		
3. Water and irrigation	9,000			
4. Game and preservation of wildlife		417		
5. Processing industry			5,500	
6. Manufacturing and construction equipment			7,270	
7. Mining and quarrying			1,800	
8. Geological mapping and mineral surveys				
9. Distribution				2,170
10. Other commerce				1,405
11. Lands and surveys				
12. Trunk roads				
13. Feeder roads				
14. Aerodromes				
15. Railways and harbors				
16. Post and telegraphs				
17. Civil aviation and meteorology				
18. Power				
19. Housing and township development				
20. Community development				
21. Labor				
22. Education				
23. Health and welfare				
24. National culture				
25. National service				
26. Law and order				
27. Defense				
28. External affairs				
29. Information services and broadcasting				
30. Government buildings				
Totals	19,373	8,226	14,570	3,575
Percentages of Total Central Government Expenditure	19.0	8.1	14.3	3.5

* Excluding uncompleted government projects from the Three Year Development Plan 1961–64 totaling approximately £6.5 million.

PUBLIC AND PRIVATE SECTORS (Monetary)*
June 1969

Government							
Infrastructure			Local Govt.				Grand Total (£000)
Economic	Social	Admin.	Monetary	Self-Help	EACSO	Private Sector	
						8,400	25,659
			100				1,023
			800				9,800
							417
						5,300	10,800
						36,000	43,270
						3,100	4,900
400							400
						13,000	15,170
						16,500	17,905
1,856			100				1,956
5,590							5,590
6,460			800	500			7,760
1,221							1,221
40					15,500		15,540
					1,000		1,000
					1,500		1,500
4,064			300				4,364
	10,448		1,300			30,000	41,748
	1,187		300	800			2,287
	199					300	499
	14,333		1,400	2,000		400	18,133
	1,805		700	700		3,000	6,205
	318						318
	725						725
		2,910					2,910
		2,300					2,300
		300					300
		400					400
		1,700	200				1,900
19,631	29,015	7,610	6,000	4,000	18,000	116,000	246,000
19.2	28.4	7.5	—	—	—	—	—

Source: Tanganyika Five Year Plan for Economic and Social Development,,
1 July, 1964–30 June, 1969.

C. THE EVOLUTION OF THE GROSS DOMESTIC PRODUCT
(£ millions)

	Actual									Target				
	1954			Average 1960-62			1970			1980		
	Monet.	Subs.	Total	Monet.	Subs.	Total	Monet.	Subs.	Total	Monet.	Subs.	Total
Crop husbandry *	29.6	40.0	69.6	37.7	45.7	83.4	72.2	54.6	126.8	123.4	65.4	188.8
Livestock *	5.9	8.4	14.3	5.9	12.3	18.2	10.6	15.1	25.7	20.9	18.8	39.7
Fishing *	1.3	0.4	1.7	1.3	0.4	1.7	2.1	0.6	2.7	3.3	0.8	4.1
Forest Products *	0.7	1.4	2.1	1.1	1.5	2.6	1.6	1.8	3.4	2.6	2.3	4.9
Mining, Quarrying	3.0	—	3.0	5.2	—	5.2	7.5	—	7.5	10.3	—	10.3
Processing and Manufacturing	5.0	—	5.0	7.4	—	7.4	25.0	—	25.0	84.9	—	84.9
Public Utilities	0.4	—	0.4	1.3	—	1.3	3.7	—	3.7	9.0	—	9.0
Construction	5.6	—	5.6	6.3	—	6.3	18.5	—	18.5	40.0	—	40.0
Transport and Comm.	5.7	—	5.7	8.7	—	8.7	17.2	—	17.2	35.8	—	35.8
Distribution	13.1	—	13.1	22.1	—	22.1	44.2	—	44.2	93.5	—	93.5
Rents and Royalties	3.5	—	3.5	8.0	—	8.0	17.0	—	17.0	33.5	—	33.5
Publ. Admin. & Def.	7.5	—	7.5	12.6	—	12.6	25.2	—	25.2	54.4	—	54.4
Other Services	3.9	—	3.9	6.9	—	6.9	15.0	—	15.0	37.2	—	37.2
Total G.D.P.	85.2	50.2	135.4	124.5	59.9	184.4	259.8	72.1	331.9	548.8	87.3	636.1
Population (millions)			8.3			6.9			11.3			14.1
Per Cap. G.D.P.			£16.3			£19.6			£29.3			£45.1

* Primary rural product for the years 1960-62 valued in 1960 prices. Other sectors' product in current prices.

Source: Tanganyika Five Year Plan for Economic and Social Development, 1 July, 1964–30 June, 1969.

D. TARGET: SECTOR RATES OF GROWTH
% (Compounded)

	1954-61			1960/62-1970			1970-1980		
	Monet.	Subs.	Total [1]	Monet.	Subs.	Total	Monet.	Subs.	Total
Crop husbandry	3.5	1.9	2.7	7.5	2.0	4.8	5.5	1.8	4.1
Livestock	0.0	5.6	3.5	6.8	2.3	3.9	6.9	2.2	4.4
Forest Product	6.7	1.0	3.1	4.3	2.2	3.2	5.0	2.2	3.7
Fishing	0.0	0.0	0.0	5.5	4.6	5.3	4.6	2.9	4.3
Mining and Quarrying			8.2			4.7			3.2
Processing and Manufacture			5.8			14.8			13.0
Public Utilities			18.8			12.3			9.3
Construction			1.7			12.7			8.0
Transport and Communications			6.8			7.8			7.6
Distribution			7.7			8.0			7.8
Rents and Royalties			12.6			8.7			7.0
Public Administration and Defense			7.6			7.9			8.0
Other Services			8.5			9.0			9.5
Total G.D.P.	5.6	2.6	4.5	8.5	2.1	6.7	7.7	2.0	6.7
Population			1.8			2.1			2.3
Per Capita Product			2.7[X]			4.6			4.3

[1] Not strictly comparable because of different sector coverage and valuation conventions.
[X] Less about 1% for annual price changes.

Source: Tanganyika Five Year Plan for Economic and Social Development, 1 July, 1964–30 June, 1969.

E. DOMESTIC EXPORTS: PRINCIPAL COMMODITIES BY QUANTITY AND VALUE AND PER CENT OF TOTAL VALUE

Commodity	1957 %	1957 Value £ 000	1958 %	1958 Value £ 000	1959 %	1959 Value £ 000	1960 %	1960 Value £ 000	1961 %	1961 Value £ 000
Sisal	24.1	9,482	24.8	10,349	28.8	13,057	28.1	15,442	28.8	14,028
Coffee	13.1	7,142	18.2	7,576	12.7	5,745	13.3	7,326	13.9	6,762
Cotton	16.7	6,578	17.4	7,249	14.7	6,657	16.1	8,827	14.0	6,794
Tea	1.5	601	1.5	632	1.7	771	2.1	1,151	2.8	1,337
Hides, skins and fur skins	3.1	1,223	2.9	1,200	4.2	1,919	3.3	1,836	3.6	1,759
Groundnuts	2.7	1,073	1.9	779	1.7	785	1.9	1,053	0.5	232
Cashew nuts	3.8	1,514	2.6	1,087	3.4	1,562	3.9	2,126	3.7	1,805
Castor seed	2.2	870	1.9	812	1.4	616	1.6	874		
Sesame seed	1.3	530	1.4	592	1.6	713	1.2	642	4.0	1,943
Other oil seeds, nuts and kernels	2.4	939	1.5	631	1.5	685	1.2	662		
Wood, lumber and cork	1.5	603	1.2	489	1.0	451	1.2	637	1.0	466
Diamonds	8.3	3,242	10.6	4,415	10.0	4,548	8.5	4,653	11.8	5,762
Gold	1.7	678	1.7	705	2.4	1,067	2.2	1,231	2.6	1,249
Lead ore and concentrates	2.9	1,129	2.1	895	1.8	829	2.0	1,077	0.2	85
Other	9.7	3,837	10.8	4,319	13.0	5,882	13.4	7,317	13.1	6,346
Total	100	39,441	100.5	41,730	99.9	45,287	100	54,854	100	48,568

Source: *Statistical Abstract*, p. 30; and *Budget Survey 62/63*, p. 14.

F. GOVERNMENT OF TANGANYIKA CAPITAL EXPENDITURES, 1948–50, 1953/56–1958/59 AND ESTIMATES FOR 1960/61

(£ 000)

Category	1948	1949	1950	1955/56	1956/57	1957/58	1958/59	1960/61 (estimates)
Economic:								
Agriculture and Animal Husbandry	169	229	359	90	72	147	247	217
Water Supplies	140	162	168	311	470	492	634	715
Roads	112	180	1,094	1,172	939	906	849	1,386
Other	71	301	113	208	85	90	140	401
Social:								
Education	47	227	292	674	1,026	1,196	1,135	677
Township Development	73	104	450	570	1,292	993	810	721
Public Health and Social Welfare	65	9	44	346	419	309	291	303
Public Buildings and Works	272	341	906	707	942	1,253	966	1,471
Other	47	134	13	6	38	68	87	289
Total	996	1,687	3,439	4,084	5,283	5,454	5,159	6,180

Source: *World Bank Report*, p. 28.

G. POSSIBLE SOURCES OF FINANCE

In line with the foregoing assumptions for the various sectors of the economy, the following tentative picture of possible sources of finance for the necessary expenditure on development has been constructed.

	Domestic			(£ millions) External		
	Self-Financing	Domestic Borrowing	Self-Help	Investment/Borrowing	Grants	Total
Central Government	8.5	14.0		71.5	8.0	102.0
Agriculture						
Irrigation and Resettlement	0.4	2.0		16.5	0.5	19.4
Traditional		1.2		6.0	1.0	8.2
Industry		2.6		12.0		14.6
Commerce		3.6				3.6
Infrastructure						
Economic	1.0	2.2		16.0	0.4	19.6
Social	1.5	0.4		21.0	6.1	29.0
Administrative	5.6	2.0				7.6
Local Government	3.5	2.5	4.0			10.0
EACSO				18.0		18.0
Government Enterprises (outside Central Budget)	1.0	8.0		12.0		21.0
Private Enterprise	72.0	4.0		15.6	3.4	95.0
Total	93.5	42.5	4.0	188.6	19.4	348.0

Source: Tanganyika Five Year Plan for Economic and Social Development, 1 July, 1964–30 June, 1969.

Appendix III

A Synopsis of Closer Union in East Africa

As this survey shows, one cannot comprehend the background of planning in Tanganyika without constant reference to East Africa generally. This transnational aspect of the politics of planning characterizes the process in Tanganyika. A synopsis of the process and politics of closer union is presented here to provide the interested reader with a more detailed and compact description of closer union.

The checkered story of the various abortive attempts to unify the East African territories tends to fall into three historical periods. The first period—from the end of the First World War to about 1931— was characterized by a campaign mounted by the European settler groups in the three territories supported by their influential sympathizers in the United Kingdom to bring about an Eastern African Dominion, dominated, of course, by the settler community. The second period witnessed the growing insistence of the Colonial Office to regard African interests as paramount and a subsequent decline in the enthusiasm of the settlers for a union they could not dominate. The period from about 1931 to 1958 was characterized by a number of attempts undertaken on the initiative of the imperial government to unify the three territories for economic and administrative purposes. Since 1958 the movement for and against closer union has passed into the hands of the Africans and has become caught up in the general pan-African movement. A chronological description of the various commissions, white papers, and reports with special emphasis on their relation to Tanganyika for our purposes will provide a relatively complete picture.

A. 1924–31

1. In 1924 the Secretary of State for the Colonies, Mr. L. S. Amery, appointed a commission under the chairmanship of the Honorable William Ormsby-Gore, M.P., to consider and report on the feasibility of closer union in East Africa. See *Ormsby-Gore Commission,* Command Paper 2387, 1924.

2. In 1925 the commission reported that it found little support for closer union in East Africa and recommended instead (among other things) periodic conferences of governors of the territories. See East Africa, *Report of the East Africa Commission,* Cmd. 2387, London, 1925.

3. In 1926 the first Conference of Governors of British East Africa met in Nairobi.

4. In 1927 the second East African Governors Conference was held in London. It was decided that a second commission should examine the question of closer union.

5. In December 1927 Mr. Amery, in a white paper entitled "Future Policy in Regard to Eastern Africa," announced the appointment of the Hilton-Young Commission under the chairmanship of Sir Edward Hilton-Young. The commission was instructed to make recommendations regarding federation or some other form of closer union in Central and East Africa.

6. In January 1929 the Hilton-Young Commission in its report accepted the idea of a closer union and went on to recommend three specific steps: (1) the appointment of a high commissioner, (2) the creation of the office of governor-general, (3) the appointment of a first governor-general with limited powers.

The report aroused so much interest and criticism both in East Africa and in the United Kingdom that the colonial secretary decided to send Sir Samuel Wilson, the Permanent Undersecretary of State for the Colonies, to East Africa to consider the recommendations of Hilton-Young and to ascertain what measure of consensus could be obtained locally for them.

7. In October 1929 the Wilson Report was released. In place of the three steps contemplated in the Hilton-Young Commission, Wilson proposed the institution of the office of high commissioner for the East African dependencies. The high commissioner was to have legislative and administrative responsibility for defined services. However, before the Wilson Report could be acted upon a change of government took place in Britain. In June 1929 the MacDonald Cabinet took over from the conservatives and was followed in 1931 by the national coalition government led by Ramsay MacDonald, which stayed in power until 1935. Lord Passfield (formerly Sidney Webb), who replaced Amery as secretary of state, effectively reversed the direction that the movement toward closer union had taken up to this point.

8. In 1930 Passfield issued two white papers: "Memorandum on the Native Policy of East Africa" and "Statement of Conclusions of His Majesty's Government in the United Kingdom as Regards Closer Union of East Africa" (Cmd. 3574). While reaffirming the inviolability of

Tanganyika as a territorial unit, and the policy of paramountcy of native interests, the Colonial Secretary agreed to the establishment of a high commissioner for East Africa. In order that the proposals should receive the fullest consideration, Passfield submitted them to the Joint Select Committee of both Houses of Parliament.

9. In 1931 the Joint Select Committee heard evidence in London on the entire question of closer union including the Hilton-Young Report, the Wilson Report, conclusions of His Majesty's Government, and evidence from governors and communal representatives of East Africa.

10. In 1931 the committee reported that it had found no support for the idea of a federation in East Africa. (See *Joint Select Committee on Closer Union in East Africa,* Vol. 1, Report, 1931, No. 184.) However, the committee accepted the need for economic cooperation and coordination among the territories concerned.

11. On December 22, 1931, in his dispatch, the Secretary of State for the Colonies informed the governors of East Africa that he had accepted the recommendations of the Joint Select Committee and that in the absence of a central authority the machinery of the Governors' Conference should be increasingly utilized for securing cooperation and coordination in all matters of common interest.

12. In April 1932, despite the fact that the Joint Select Committee did not approve closer union, the Conference of East African Governors approved a project for the unification of the posts and telegraphs administration to come into effect in January 1933.

13. On July 13, 1932, another dispatch from the Colonial Office stated that no far-reaching steps in the direction of the formal union of the territories should be taken at that time.

4. In March 1948 the first East African Central Assembly sat.

5. In January 1953 the East African Royal Commission was appointed under the chairmanship of Sir Hugh Dow to examine measures required to improve the standard of living in East Africa with reference to land use and resources. In its report the commission concluded that East Africa as a region could best be developed as a single unit. (See East Africa, *Royal Commission 1953–55 Report,* Cmd. 7475, p. 269.)

6. In July 1953, as the Royal Commission began its work in East Africa, the Colonial Secretary, Mr. Oliver Lyttelton (later Lord Chandos), at an East African dinner party, alluded to the inevitable "evolution as time goes on, of still larger measures of unification and possibly still larger measures of federation of the whole of East African territories." This statement set off a constitutional crisis leading to the exile of the Kabaka of Buganda. (See Cmd. 9828, p. 6.)

7. In July 1960 the Secretary of State for the Colonies appointed a commission headed by Jeremy Raisman "to examine arrangements at present in force in East Africa for a common market area, for economic coordination between territories and for fiscal uniformity." The Raisman Report appeared in January 1961. The Raisman Commission reported that the foundations of the Common Market in East Africa preceded the establishment of the High Commission by many years and may be said to have been laid in 1917, when free trade between Uganda and Kenya was first established.

Tanganyika became a part of this embryonic common market by stages: a common external tariff was adopted in 1922; free interchange of domestic products with Kenya and Uganda was inaugurated in 1923; free transfer of imported goods followed in 1927. But the Tanganyika Customs Department was not amalgamated with that of the other two territories until 1949. (See East Africa, *Report of the Economic and Fiscal Commission,* Cmd. 1279, p. 9.)

8. In June 1961 discussions in England on the future of the High Commission Services in an independent East Africa resulted in the formation of the present East African Common Services Organization which replaced the East African High Commission. (See Colonial Office, *The Future of East Africa High Commission Services,* Cmd. 1433, July 1961.)

C. THE PAN-AFRICAN ASPECT OF EAST AFRICAN FEDERATION

1. In September 1958 at Mwanza, Tanganyika, delegates from the East African territories met and drafted a "Freedom Charter" pledging themselves to the achievement of African freedom throughout the

continent. They established at this meeting the Pan-African Freedom Movement of East and Central Africa, PAFMECA.

2. In September 1959 the second PAFMECA conference was held at Moshi, Tanganyika.

3. In October 1960 the third annual conference of PAFMECA was held at Mbale, Uganda.

4. In January 1961 the fourth annual conference was held in Nairobi. This conference called for the establishment of a Federation of East Africa on the attainment of self-government and the breaking up of the present white-dominated Federation of Rhodesia and Nyasaland so as to enable those territories to join their East African neighbors. In their final resolution the delegates affirmed that

> a federation was politically and economically essential, that it could only be brought about by elected and African controlled governments and that . . . such governments should then confer and work the details of the federation and that no reactionary and imperialist elements should interfere with the designing of the federation and that it should be left to the Africans.

5. The fifth annual PAFMECA conference was held in February 1962 at Addis Ababa, Ethiopia.

Here delegates pledged to work relentlessly for a federation of Eastern Africa as soon as Kenya, Uganda, and Zanzibar attained their independence. Under its new name, PAFMECSA, the organization foresaw a federation embracing not only East Africa, Ethiopia, and Somalia but possibly Central and South Africa as well. Toward this end the conference called upon the East African Common Services Organization (EACSO) and the governments of Ethiopia and Somalia to begin immediate discussions on the extension of the East African Common Market and EACSO to embrace these two states as well. The need for cooperative efforts in the fields of transportation and communication was given special emphasis. (See *Africa Report,* Vol. 7, March 1962, p. 14.)

Since 1958 Tanganyika has played a leading role in the various attempts to federate East Africa. Indeed, it was Julius Nyerere who initiated PAFMECA when he called the first meeting of East African leaders in 1958. In 1960 Dr. Nyerere indicated he even was willing to postpone the date for Tanganyika's independence if this could help the formation of an East African Federation. Today, after attainment of independence, evidence seems to indicate that most Tanganyikan leaders are still committee to the formation of an East African Federation.

6. A PAFMECSA conference was held in Leopoldville in December 1962 to further the integration of the Congo and explore the possibility of economic association of East and Central Africa with the Congo.

†††

Notes

I. The Setting for Planning

1. J. P. Moffett, ed. (Dar es Salaam: Government Printer, 1958), p. 34.

2. The most infamous engagement was that of the Maji-Maji rebellion of 1905–1907. The indigenous peoples of the Southern Province engaged in a desperate struggle against the technologically superior German forces. The rebellion was finally put down but at a terrible price with an estimated 120,000 Africans having died as a direct or indirect consequence of the ruthlessness of the German repression. The Southern Province never has fully recovered from this incident and the poverty and scarce population are in part a legacy of this unfortunate chapter of German colonialism.

3. Moffett, p. 81.

II. Engagement—To Plan Is Not to Plan

1. Moffett, p. 91.

2. *Ibid.,* p. 92.

3. German administration, in contrast to the British, was "direct" and was established in many instances on the ruins of indigenous tribal governing systems, not unlike those employed with great effectiveness in the implementation of indirect rule by the British in Uganda.

4. For a comprehensive treatment of this subject, see U. K. Hicks, *Development from Below* (New York: Oxford University Press, 1961).

5. *Tanganyika Annual Report 1920.*

6. *Tanganyika Annual Report 1936,* as quoted in Moffett, p. 113.

7. Moffett, p. 96.

8. Babu Niculescu, *Colonial Planning: A Comparative Study* (London: George Allen and Unwin, 1958), p. 39.

9. *Ibid.*

10. Sydney Armitage-Smith, *Report of a Financial Mission to Tanganyika,* C.M.O. 4182 (London: H.M.S.O., 1947).

III. The Wartime Crisis and the Genesis of Planning

1. From 1930 to 1940 approximately twelve million pounds were granted "to cover budget deficits for extraordinary expenditures in the colonies." Niculescu, p. 57.

2. *Ibid.*, p. 58.

3. *Ibid.*, p. 63.

4. *Ibid.*

5. For a chronology of federation politics see Appendix 3.

6. World Bank, *The Economic Development of Tanganyika* (Baltimore: Johns Hopkins Press, 1961), p. 133. Hereinafter cited as *World Bank Report.*

7. *Hansard,* 27 February 1948.

8. Elspeth Huxley, *The Sorcerer's Apprentice* (London: Chatto and Windus, 1956), p. 140.

9. Moffett, p. 133.

10. George Kimble, *Tropical Africa* (2 vols.; New York: Twentieth Century Fund, 1960), vol. I, p. 173.

11. Moffett, p. 135.

12. Kimble, I, p. 173.

13. Huxley, p. 136.

14. Moffett, p. 135.

15. T. T. G. Chidzero, *Tanganyika and International Trusteeship* (London: Oxford University Press, 1961), p. 235.

16. Lord Hailey, *An African Survey Revised 1956* (London: Oxford University Press, 1957), p. 1296.

17. *Ibid.*

18. *A Memorandum* prepared by TAC for the World Bank, Mimeographed, June 1959, p. 1, quoted in Kimble, I. p. 174.

19. See *World Bank Report*, pp. 222–226.

20. *Ibid.*

21. Tanganyika Agricultural Corporation, *Report and Accounts 1958–59* (Dar es Salaam: Government Printer), 1960.

22. *World Bank Report*, p. 224.

23. *Ibid.*

24. *Ibid.*

IV. Planned Disengagement—Politics and Process

1. Anthony Rweyemamu, "Preparations for Independence in Tanganyika," Unpublished Master's Thesis, University of Nebraska, 1962, p. 39.

2. *Report of the UN Visiting Mission to Tanganyika,* 1948, T/218 ADV 1, p. 2.

3. For an excellent discussion of this problem see Karl Deutsch, *Nationalism and Social Communication* (New York: John Wiley, 1953).

4. *Report of the U.N. Visiting Mission to Tanganyika,* 1951, BOCT/ 946, p. 42.

5. Statement in defense of the Preventive Detention Act of 1962, *Daily Nation,* Sept. 28, 1962, p. 1.

6. Rweyemamu, p. 16.

7. *Ibid.*

8. *Ibid.,* p. 34.

9. Final decision in all matters, including financial of course, rested with the governor. When acting contrary to the advice of the Executive Council, the governor, by custom, was required to report the circumstances to the secretary of state for the colonies.

10. *Proposals of the Tanganyika Government for a Republic: Government Paper No. 1, 1962* (Dar es Salaam: Government Printer, 1962).

11. *Times* (London) Supplement, December 9, 1962, p. vi; *Budget Survey 1962–63,* p. 4; the *World Bank Report* estimates per capita money income at 6 pounds, p. 16. Gross national product in 1954 was 80.8 million pounds; 1955, 84.5 million; 1956, 87.4 million; 1957, 92.7 million; in 1957, per capita income was 48 dollars in Tanganyika whereas in Uganda it was 57 dollars and in Kenya 78 dollars. *Economic Survey of Africa Since 1950,* United Nations, E/CN, p. 77.

12. *Conference of East African Governors; Report of a Fiscal Survey of Kenya, Uganda and Tanganyika,* Sir Wilfrid Woods, August 1, 1946, Colonial 349. Tax revenue exclusive of import and excise duties in 1958/59 was more than 6.5 million pounds. *World Bank Report,* p. 24.

13. Woods, p. 145.

14. Niculescu, p. 99.

15. Until 1948 and the establishment of the East African High Commission, the Tanganyika railroad was the responsibility solely of Tanganyika; after that date it was joined by those of Uganda and Kenya and came under the control of the East African High commission.

16. The World Bank Mission recommended 18 million pounds. See *World Bank Report,* p. 35; Development Plan for Tanganyika 1961/62– 1963/64 (Dar es Salaam: Government Printer, 1961). It is anticipated that the development plan will be met by the addition of grants and loans from Britain of 13 million pounds, a loan from West Germany in excess of 3 million pounds, and an American loan of approximately 3.5 million pounds.

17. Tanganyika's Five Year Plan for Economic and Social Development (Dar es Salaam: Government Printer, April 1964), especially Vol. I, pp. 95–110, Financial Aspects of the Plan. See appendix of detailed allocations.

18. *An act to establish the Tanganyika Development Corporation,* Government Notice 20 of 1962, 11 July 1962.

19. The West German government has offered Tanganyika a total of 4.2 million dollars in grants and technical aid. The increasing cooperation of West Germany in Tanganyika, in the latter's development, is also demonstrated by the provision of technical assistance, including placing at the disposal of the Tanganyika government a general planning adviser and three town plan specialists.

20. *Tanganyika Industrial Development—A Preliminary Study of Bases for the Expansion of Industrial Processing Activities,* December 1961, C-63989.

21. *Budget Survey 1962/63* (Dar es Salaam: Government Printer), p. 2.

22. *Ibid.*

23. "Uhuru Na What?" *Spearhead,* Vol. I, No. 2, December 1961, p. 3.

24. *Development Plan for Tanganyika 1961/62–1963/64.*

25. Huxley, p. 40.

26. *World Bank Report,* p. 34.

27. *Development Plan for Tanganyika 1961/62–1963/64,* p. 14.

28. W. Kalpish, "Industrial Prospects," *Spearhead,* Vol. I, No. 2, December 1961, p. 16.

29. *Ibid.*

30. *Ibid.*

31. *Ibid.*

32. *World Bank Report,* p. 61.

33. *Spearhead,* Vol. I, No. 2, December 1961.

34. *World Bank Report,* p. 61.

35. Given the rapid changes in locality governance taking place throughout Tanganyika, it is likely today for some regions that the support of the local government council or local TANU leader will be required. It is the policy of the Tanganyika government to divest chiefs of all but their purely ceremonial and tradition-oriented functions and replace them with civil officers.

36. Nyerere's statement to the press announcing his resignation. See *Times* (London), January 23, 1962, p. 10.

37. Moffett, p. 117.

38. British Information Services, *Tanganyika, Making of a Nation,* 1961, p. 15.

39. *Ibid.*

40. *World Bank Report,* p. 121.

41. *KNCU Annual Report 1960–61.*

42. Moffett, p. 212.

43. Partly accounted for by the fact that community development (formerly social development) up to mid-1962 was a part of the Ministry of Local Government.

44. *Tanganyika, Making of a Nation,* p. 42.

Selected Bibliography

UNITED KINGDOM GOVERNMENT PUBLICATIONS

*Command
Papers, No.:*

1922 Statement of Policy on East Africa, 1922.
2387 Ormsby-Gore Commission, 1924.
3234 Report of Closer Union Commission (Hilton-Young), 1929.
3573 Memo on Native Policy, 1929.
3574 Statement of Conclusions of H.M. Government in the United Kingdom as Regards Closer Union of East Africa, 1930.
3378 Report of Sir Samuel Wilson, 1929.
4141 Correspondence Arising from Committee on Closer Union, 1931.
4182 Financial Mission to Tanganyika (Sir S. Armitage-Smith), 1932.
4235 Report on Railway Tariffs (Mr. Gibb), 1932.
6174 Royal Commission on the West Indies, 1939.
6175 Statement of Policy on Colonial Development and Welfare, 1940.
6299 Certain Aspects of Colonial Policy during War-time, 1941.
6457 Report on the Operation of the C.D. & W. Act 1942, 1942.
6532 Report on the Operation of the C.D. & W. Act 1942, 1944.
6713 Dispatch from Secretary of State to Colonial Governments, November 12, 1945.
7030 Plan for Mechanized Production of Groundnuts in East and Central Africa, 1944.
9375 Report on the Administration and Use of Funds Provided under C.D. & W. Acts, 1955.
9462 Colonial Development and Welfare Act, April 26, 1955.
9475 Royal Commission Report on East Africa, 1955.
9769 Report on the Administration and Use of Funds Provided under C.D. & W. Acts, 1956.
9801 Despatches from East African Governors on Royal Commission Report, 1956.
9804 Commentary on Despatches from East African Governors, 1956.
1360 Report of the Tanganyika Constitutional Conference, 1961.
1433 Future of East African High Commission Services, 1961.

Colonial
Papers, No.:

57 Papers Relating to the Question of Closer Unions of Kenya, Uganda and Tanganyika Territory, 1931.
81 Report of Railway Advisory Council for East Africa, 1933.
312 Memo of Postwar Problems in East Africa, 1943.
191 Inter-Territorial Organization in East Africa, 1945.
3 Development Planning (Anexure to Cmd. 6713), 1945.
210 Inter-Territorial Organization in East Africa, Revised Proposal, 1947.
277 Development of African Local Government in Tanganyika, 1951.
191 Report on East African Organizations, 1952.
290 Land and Population in East Africa, 1952.
239 United Kingdom's Role in Commonwealth Development, 1957.
281 An Economic Survey of Colonial Territories, 1957.

TANGANYIKA DEVELOPMENT PLANS

Report of Central Development Committee, 1940.
An Outline of Post War Development Proposals, 1944.
A Ten Year Development and Welfare Plan for Tanganyika Territory, 1946.
Revised Development Plan, 1950–1956, 1950.
Review of Development in Southern Province, 1953.
Five Year Development and Capital Works Programs, 1955.
Revision of Five Year Development Plan, 1957.
Development Plan for Tanganyika 1961/62–1963/64.
Tanganyika's Five Year Plan for Economic and Social Development 1964–1969, 1964.

OTHER TANGANYIKA PUBLICATIONS

Agricultural Development Reports, 1919–1961.
Tanganyika Annual Report, 1919–1961.
Report of Committee on Customs Tariff, 1922.
Land Ordinance, 1923.
Report on Indirect Administration, 1925.
Report of Customs Tariff and Railway Rates Committee, Entebbe, 1929.
Report of the Railway Commission (Sir S. Henn), 1930.
Notes on Customs Policy, 1933.
Revised Plan of the Overseas Food Corporation, 1949.
Report of Central African Survey (Sir A. Gibb & Partners), 1952.
Overseas Economic Survey, British East Africa, 1952.
Cotton Industry, 1939–1953, 1953.

Commission on Constituitonal Development (Professor W. J. M. Mac-Kenzie), 1953.
A Plan to Intensify the Development of African Agriculture in Kenya (Suynnerton), 1954.
National Income Accounts, 1954–57.
Report of Committee on East African Railways Road Service, 1954.
Tanganyika: A Review of Its Resources and Their Development, 1955.
British Information Services, *Economic Development in the Commonwealth,* I.D. 13, 1956.
Tanganyika Annual Report of the Department of Commerce and Industry, 1958.
Tanganyika Agricultural Corporation: Report and Account for 1958–1959, 1960.
Statistical Abstract, Series 1938–1960, 1960.
Tanganyika: The Making of a Nation, I.D. 1386, 1961.
Commerce and Industry in Tanganyika, 1961.
Tanganyika Industrial Development, December, 1961, Arthur D. Little, Inc.
Budget Survey 1962–63, Tanganyika Trade Journal.

UNITED NATIONS PUBLICATIONS

United Nations. *African Statistics, Economic Bulletin for Africa,* June 1961.
United Nations. *Economic Bulletin for Africa,* June 1961.
United Nations. *Economic Survey of Africa Since 1950.*
United Nations. *Trusteeship Council: Administrative Unions Affecting Trust Territories: First Report of the Standing Committee on Administrative Unions: Tanganyika,* U.N. Doc. T/915, June 5, 1951.
United Nations. *Trusteeship Council, Official Records: Reports of the U.N. Visiting Missions to East Africa, on Tanganyika.*

1948, Doc. T/218
1951, Doc. T/946
1954, Doc. T/1142
1957, Doc. T/1345
1960, Doc. T/1532

BOOKS

Banks, A. L. *Development of Tropical and Subtropical Countries, with Particular Reference to Africa.* New York: St. Martins Press, 1955.
Bisset, C. B. *Minerals and Industry in Tanganyika.* London: Her Majesty's Stationery Office, 1955.

Braibanti, R. and J. J. Spengler. *Tradition, Values, and Socio-economic Development*. Durham: Duke University Press, 1961.

Cameron, Sir Donald. *My Tanganyika Service and Some Nigeria*. London: Allen and Unwin, 1939.

Chidzero, T. T. G. *Tanganyika and International Trusteeship*. London: Oxford University Press, 1961.

Dow-Smith, A. T. *British East Africa: Economic and Commercial Conditions*. London: Her Majesty's Stationery Office, 1953.

Economist (London periodical). *Commonwealth and Europe*. London: Economist Intelligence Unit, 1960.

Economist Intelligence Unit (for East African Railways & Harbors). *The Economy of East Africa: A Study of Trends*. Nairobi, 1955.

Ford, V. E. R. *The Trade of Lake Victoria*. East African Studies Series No. 3. Kampala: East African Institute of Social Research, 1955.

Frankel, S. H. *Economic Impact on Underdeveloped Societies*. Oxford: Basil Blackwell, 1953.

————. *Some Aspects of Investment and Economic Development in the Continent of Africa*. London: Oxford University Press, 1952.

Hailey, Lord. *An African Survey*. London: Oxford University Press, 1957 (revised edition).

Hicks, U. *Development from Below*. New York: Oxford University Press, 1957.

Hill, M. F. *Permanent Way: The Story of the Kenya and Uganda Railway*. Nairobi: East African Railways and Harbors, 1950.

———— and J. P. Moffett. *Review of Resources and Their Development*. Dar es Salaam: Government Printer, 1955.

Huxley, E. *The Sorcerer's Apprentice*. London: Chatto and Windus, 1956.

Kimble, G. *Tropical Africa,* Vol. 1. New York: Twentieth Century Fund, 1960.

Leubuscher, C. *Bulk Buying from the Colonies*. London: Oxford University Press, 1956.

————. *Tanganyika Territory: A Study of Economic Policy under Mandate*. London: Oxford University Press, 1944.

Moffett, J. P. *Handbook of Tanganyika*. Dar es Salaam: Government Printer, 1958.

Molohan, M. J. B. *Detribalization*. Dar es Salaam: Government Printer, 1959.

Newlyn, W. T. and D. C. Rowan. *Money and Banking in British Colonial Africa*. Oxford-Clarendon Press, 1954.

Niculescu, B. *Colonial Planning*. London: Allen and Unwin, 1958.

Peacock, A. T. and D. G. M. Dosser. *National Income of Tanganyika,*

1952–1954, Colonial Research Study No. 26. London: Her Majesty's Stationery Office, 1958.

Rweyemamu, A. H. "Preparations for Independence in Tanganyika." Unpublished Master's Thesis, University of Nebraska, 1962.

Woods, Sir Wilfrid. *Conference of East African Governors Report on a Fiscal Survey of Kenya, Uganda and Tanganyika.* Nairobi: East African Governor's Council, 1946.

World Bank. *The Economic Development of Tanganyika.* Baltimore: The Johns Hopkins Press, 1961.

ARTICLES

Africa Today, VIII (December 1961).

Cory, H. "Reforms of Tribal Political Institutions in Tanganyika." *Journal of African Administration,* XII (April 1960), pp. 77–84.

Darby, Anthony. "East Africa." *The New Commonwealth,* XXXIX (February 1961), pp. 74–78.

————. "East Africa: The Case for Federation." *The New Commonwealth,* XXXIX (March 1961), pp. 144–47.

Dobson, E. B. "Comparative Land Tenure of Ten Tanganyika Tribes." *Tanganyika Notes and Records,* XXXVIII (Dar es Salaam, March 1955).

Gillman, C. A. "Short History of Tanganyika Railways." *Tanganyika Notes and Records* (Dar es Salaam, June 1952).

————. "Dar es Salaam, 1860 to 1940: A Story of Growth and Change." *Tanganyika Notes and Records* (Dar es Salaam, 1945).

Keith, Robert C. "Self-Rule in Tanganyika." *Africa Special Report,* IV (November 1960).

Liebenow, Gus Se., Jr. "Responses to Planned Political Change in Tanganyika Tribal Groups." *American Political Science Review,* L (June 1956).

Lowenkopf, Martin. "Outlook for Tanganyika." *Africa Report,* VI (December 1961), pp. 3–6.

Nyerere, J. K. "We Cannot Afford to Fail." *Africa Special Report,* IV (1960).

Pratt, C. "Multiracialism and Local Government in Tanganyika." *Race,* XI (November 1960).

Soper, T. "Africa Links with Europe after Independence." *Optima* (September 1960).

Sutton, Francis X. "Planning and Rationality in Newly Independent States of Africa." *Economic Development and Cultural Change,* X (October 1960).

Index

105